REV TOBIAS HARTWELL

ST. MARTIN DE PORRES

His Life, His Miracles, His Legacy Of Love.

Copyright © 2024 by REV TOBIAS HARTWELL

All rights reserved. No part of this publication may be reproduced, stored or transmitted in any form or by any means, electronic, mechanical, photocopying, recording, scanning, or otherwise without written permission from the publisher. It is illegal to copy this book, post it to a website, or distribute it by any other means without permission.

REV TOBIAS HARTWELL asserts the moral right to be identified as the author of this work.

First edition

*This book was professionally typeset on Reedsy.
Find out more at reedsy.com*

To those who serve without acknowledgment, those with caring hearts who cross borders, and those seeking universal love.

May the life of St. Martin de Porres encourage you to live with courage, compassion, and unfailing faith.

This book is dedicated to everyone who believes in the transformative power of love, as well as those who, like Martin, choose to travel the road of humility in a world that frequently ignores it.

May his tale inspire you.

Contents

Introduction	1
HUMBLE BEGINNINGS IN LIMA	3
A Life Shaped by Humility	3
Discovering a Calling	6
The Struggles of a Young Soul	10
Embracing Service Over Status	15
THE PATH TO HOLINESS	19
Choosing a Life of Poverty.	19
Devotion to the Sick and Needy	23
Miraculous Moments of Mercy	27
Transforming Lives through Compassion	31
THE HEART OF A HEALER	35
Healing Hands, Divine Gifts	35
Faith in the Midst of Suffering	39
Miraculous Cures and Encounters	43
The Gift of Inner Peace.	47
ENDURING TRIALS WITH FAITH	51
Bearing the Cross of Prejudice	51
Faith in the Flames of Adversity	55
The Power of Forgiveness	58
Perseverance in Prayer	62
THE MIRACLES AND MYSTERIES OF ST. MARTIN	66
Visions and Spiritual Encounters	66
Miracles of Multiplication and Provision.	70
Breaking the Laws of Nature	73
A Living Witness of Divine Love	77

LEGACY OF LOVE AND MERCY ... 81
    A Heart for All Creation ... 81
    Unity and Harmony in Community ... 84
    Patron to the Poor and Forgotten ... 88
    A Legacy Carved with Love ... 91
CANONIZATION AND THE MODERN DEVOTION TO ST. MARTIN ... 95
    The Journey to Sainthood ... 95
    Celebrating the Feast Day of St. Martin ... 98
    Miracles of St. Martin Today ... 102
    A Model of Faith for Our Time ... 106

Introduction

- **A SAINT FOR EVERYONE**

A lowly kid was born in the heart of Lima, Peru, amid the churning currents of colonial injustice and racial divide, leaving a legacy that would transcend time and place, inspiring millions around the world. St. Martin de Porres, the son of a Spanish nobleman and a liberated African slave, grew up in a world where social hierarchies governed his every action. Despite this adversity, Martin fashioned a life of amazing grace, humility, and compassion, becoming a beacon of light for the underprivileged and a living testament to God's unending love.

Martin's narrative is not one of royal birth or great accomplishments but of profound service, self-sacrifice, and heavenly favor. In a world that frequently prioritizes power, wealth, and position, St. Martin's path was marked by a steadfast dedication to the poor, sick, and forgotten. His life was not about pursuing personal glory but about pouring out his love for others in a quiet, invisible way that caught the attention of Heaven.

As a Dominican friar, Martin was known not just for his intense spiritual commitment but also for his extraordinary compassion, as he performed miracles that no one could explain. His healing touch, concern for animals and the environment, and ability to bridge racial and socioeconomic gaps made him a saint for all people, regardless of background or status.

This book takes us on a trip through the life of St. Martin de Porres, inspiring and challenging us to see the world through the eyes of compassion, humility, and grace rather than the divisions of race, class, and culture. As we journey with Martin through his trials, successes, and moments of divine contact, we will realize that holiness is not reserved for a chosen few but is attainable to all of us, no matter where we begin or where we end up.

St. Martin's story challenges us to evaluate the institutions in our own lives. It challenges us to reconsider what true greatness is and how we, too, may make a difference in the lives of others. In a world starving for hope, his example serves as a reminder that every act of kindness, no matter how tiny, has the potential to alter the world.

In the pages that follow, you will learn not just the historical facts about his life but also the spiritual depth that still resonates with us now. You will see the heart of a man who chose love over position, service over power, and compassion over conflict. As you read, may your own heart be motivated to live a life of greater love, humility, and service, as St. Martin did many years before.

Finally, Martin's life demonstrates a profound truth, holiness is not defined by the praises we receive or the titles we hold. It is about how we love, serve, and let God's grace light through our lives, illuminating the world for all to see.

HUMBLE BEGINNINGS IN LIMA

A Life Shaped by Humility

In the bustling, energetic streets of Lima, Peru, during the late 16th century, a small child named Martin de Porres was born into circumstances that, to many, appeared less than promising. The complexity of Martin's lineage and the deeply ingrained social boundaries of the time overshadowed his birth on December 9, 1579. He was the illegitimate child of a Spanish lord, Don Juan de Porres, and a freed African lady, Ana Velázquez. This mixed lineage pushed him to the periphery of society from infancy, but it was precisely in this poor beginning that the seeds of Martin's amazing humility and faith took root.

Martin, a youngster of African and Spanish origin, had to deal with the harsh reality of racial prejudice and social isolation. In Lima's stratified culture, his dark skin identified him as an outsider, relegating him to the margins of a community that valued ancestry and appearance above all else. Martin, unlike his father, inherited his mother's skin, and as a result, Don Juan struggled to embrace his son, only hesitantly recognizing him. Growing up, Martin experienced the sting of rejection not only from society but also from his own blood. It was a wound that could have rendered him bitter, but Martin learned to accept the humility that such circumstances put on him.

Despite the difficulties, Martin's mother, Ana, remained a constant presence in his life. She was a genuinely spiritual woman whose strength in the face of suffering inspired young Martin. Ana worked tirelessly as a laundress to provide for Martin and his younger sister, Juana, instilling in them a strong sense of faith and determination. Martin learned at a young age the value of hard labor and the dignity it imparted, regardless of one's social standing. This lesson would mold Martin's perspective, instilling a respect for labor and a heart sensitive to the plight of the oppressed.

During those early years, Martin developed a quiet strength—a commitment forged not by privilege but by adversity and prayer. Ana would gather her children in their little, poor house and lead them in daily prayer. The glimmer of candles lighted their humble abode, forming gentle shadows on the walls as they repeated prayers and trusted God to guide them through the day. Martin began to develop a great love for God while kneeling with his mother, a love that would evolve into a strong devotion that would guide him throughout his life.

Martin's character emerged from modest, invisible moments of service and humility rather than big shows of money or power. From a young age, he had profound empathy for others, particularly those who, like him, were excluded by society. As he traversed the small streets of Lima, he noticed the lives of the impoverished, the sick, and the homeless. He recognized in them mirrors of his own challenges, and instead of despair, he felt a passionate compassion that would come to define his ministry. In each face, he began to perceive Christ's likeness, a discovery that would serve as a guiding principle in his life and work.

Despite his youth, Martin was wise beyond his years, frequently seeking peace and insight via prayer. He would spend hours in contemplation, attracted to God as if by an invisible thread of grace. This early prayer habit served as a haven for him, a place where the sorrow of rejection receded and God's acceptance engulfed him. In those peaceful moments, Martin realized a vital truth: his worth was not based on cultural approval but on God's unconditional love for him. This revelation was both liberating and transforming for him, allowing him to see humility as a source of power rather than defeat.

Despite his growing faith, Martin could not escape the realities of his socioeconomic situation. As he grew older, he was placed in an apprenticeship with a local barber-surgeon, which is a popular job for people of mixed origin. Martin embraced the low-status post graciously, seeing it as an opportunity to help others. Martin learned the arts of medicine from the barber-surgeon, which would later become an important component of his ministry. He tirelessly trained the profession, not for personal benefit but because he wanted to serve those in need. In his hands, healing became an act of love, a method to reflect God's mercy on the hurting.

Martin's humility grew deeper as a result of his early experiences. Unlike others who might dislike such a poor position, he saw it as a blessing, an opportunity to emulate Christ's humility. He saw his hands as tools for God's work, blessed not by their skill but by their desire to offer comfort and relief. Martin never sought credit or accolades; instead, he served quietly, preferring to be in the background. In a society that valued money and honor, Martin's life was a silent monument to the power of humility, a virtue that would elevate him to sainthood in the eyes of the Church and those he served.

Martin would retreat to prayer at night after a long day of work, seeking God's guidance and strength. His prayers were modest and spoken with humility. He prayed not for money or esteem but for the ability to serve, love, and forgive. Martin's soul was renewed every night as he kneeled in prayer, and his mission was confirmed. He understood that his life was not his own and that he was destined to be a servant in the deepest sense, a conduit of God's love in a world often lacking compassion.

Meanwhile, Martin put his sympathy into each small act he could perform. Working as a barber-surgeon had given him skills that were beneficial to the suffering poor, so he began treating everyone in need, frequently for free. He repaired wounds, prescribed herbal treatments, and comforted the sick with patience and gentleness that made an indelible impression on everyone he touched. Even as an apprentice, he had an almost mystical capacity to comfort the sick, and people began to seek him out, not only for his healing abilities but also for the kindness and solace he offered. Martin's name grew gradually around Lima, whispering among those who had no other source of relief.

These early acts of kindness revealed the beginnings of his vocation. Martin saw assisting others as a natural extension of his nature, not something he did reluctantly or proudly. He saw in each sufferer a soul worthy of love and respect, and he treated them as he would Christ himself. He saw every wound as an opportunity to show God's love, every illness as an opportunity to soothe, and every moment of suffering as a method to gain empathy. With each soft touch and murmured prayer, Martin's calling became clearer—not only to himself but also to those who came to rely on him.

One day, after treating a homeless guy on the street, Martin felt compelled to enter the church and give a prayer of thankfulness. In the calm shadows of the chapel, he kneeled before the altar, his heart full with gratitude and optimism. He prayed earnestly, asking God to direct his steps and show him how to serve more fully. As he prayed, a deep serenity flowed over him, assuring him that, despite the challenges he faced, he was precisely where he needed to be. For Martin, this moment of surrender was important—a silent commitment to a life entirely dedicated to God's service.

Martin's effort eventually drew the attention of the Dominican friars, who were pleased by his humility and dedication. Though they could not take him fully into the order due to his past, they welcomed him as a lay helper, allowing him to labor inside the monastery while fulfilling his calling in a modest and inconspicuous manner. Martin accepted this position without protest or hesitation, content just to be among those who shared his aim for a life of service. He considered himself not as a lesser person for being a lay assistant but as fortunate to have any function at all in the community he valued.

As he began his duties in the monastery, Martin maintained the humility and love that had marked him since childhood. He cleaned the friars' quarters, prepared their meals, and cared for the monastery's animals without feeling resentful or proud. Martin saw every duty as an opportunity to strengthen his relationship with God, whether it was sweeping floors or caring for the sick who sought sanctuary at the monastery's doors. He considered every modest task as an act of devotion, and it filled his heart with joy merely to serve.

Martin's healing abilities quickly gained recognition among the friars. His understanding of herbal treatments, along with his innate compassion, made him a great resource for the monastery's infirmary. Word of his abilities spread to the monastery's head, who recognized Martin as more than just a helper but as a man uniquely tuned to God's work. Though Martin was still technically forbidden from joining the Order as a full brother, the friars began to look to him for advice and knowledge on care and healing, a witness to his undeniable grace in dealing with everyone and everything.

Despite these minor accolades, Martin remained sincerely humble, never letting his reputation overwhelm his devotion to God's plan. He continued to consider himself a humble servant, carrying out God's will as best he could with the resources at his disposal. Martin realized that his gifts were not for his personal glory but for the benefit of others, and he never hesitated to lend his skills to anyone in need, whether they were rich or poor, noble or pariah. His unwavering humility and compassion served as the cornerstone for his ministry, which would go on to become famous throughout Peru.

Martin's contacts with the Dominican Order and early acts of kindness brought him closer to God, and his vocation unfolded with each step he took. He may not have been approved as a full member of the Order, but he recognized that his calling was to serve in whatever form God provided. For Martin, the simple act of giving up his own aspirations in favor of God's plan provided him with joy and peace that worldly honors could not provide. His life was beginning to take shape, distinguished by an unyielding commitment to humility, compassion, and the quiet, consistent fulfillment of his calling.

The Struggles of a Young Soul

As Martin settled into his post at the Dominican monastery, his spirit soared with thankfulness, but the outside world presented persistent obstacles that tested his faith and resilience. The facts of his mixed background and poor station weighed heavily on him every day, yet he bore them with quiet dignity, preferring humility and forgiveness over resentment. Lima was a city of immense cultural and ethnic richness, but society's structures remained strict and unyielding, especially towards people of African origin like Martin. His encounters with intolerance only increased his reliance on God, as he learned to navigate an environment that seemed to offer him little acceptance outside the walls of the monastery. Each experience with discrimination was a test of his character, forcing him to rely more heavily on his faith and seek solace in God's plan, even when his heart was heavy.

Martin's youth was defined by experiences that exposed society's perception of him as "lesser," moments that may have destroyed a weaker spirit. Despite his modest demeanor and devotion, he was treated harshly and dismissively by people who thought they were superior. He was frequently ridiculed by both the wealthy and others who saw his humble status as a source of shame. Many perceived his African heritage not only as a physical characteristic but also as an underlying defect, a barrier that made him unworthy of honor or respect. People openly displayed their prejudice, viewing him with distrust or disdain, questioning his intents and talents merely on the basis of his skin color and birth circumstances.

Though Martin had sought safety at the monastery, his situation remained one that society regarded only as appropriate for individuals on the outskirts. As a lay helper, he was allowed to work, serve, and pray, but only from the sidelines. He could clean the friars' quarters, care for the animals, and assist in the infirmary, but he was not recognized as a "brother" by the church or by certain members of the monastery. While the majority of the friars admired Martin's dedication, a few were uneasy in his company, unable to see beyond the prejudices they had acquired from a society steeped in inflexible conceptions about race and position. To them, he was a servant and a helper, but never an equal.

Despite these unpleasant realities, Martin chose not to let bitterness grow in his heart. Instead, he saw each adversity as an opportunity to develop virtue. For Martin, brushes with discrimination were painful reminders of his station in the world, but he saw them as a call to humility and tolerance. In times of hurt, he turned to prayer, asking God for the grace to react with kindness and forgiveness, even to those who had wronged him. Martin had a strong faith in God's divine design and was confident that his trials were not in vain. Every day, he opted to embrace his burdens, offering them as quiet sacrifices in solidarity with Christ's own suffering, which provided him with the fortitude to go through each challenge.

However, there were occasions when his struggles felt almost terrible. Martin's spirit was soft, highly compassionate, and sensitive to the suffering of others; nonetheless, he carried a silent agony within himself, a sense of being marked apart, not for his virtues but for attributes beyond his control. He frequently questioned why God had permitted him to suffer so many challenges and why his life had been filled with rejection and misery. In his alone, he posed these issues to God, seeking answers in the silence of prayer. And, while he rarely received a direct response, he felt God's presence near to him, reassuring him that he was never alone.

In the midst of his tribulations, Martin realized that his trials were shaping him in ways he could not have predicted. The humility he developed in response to other people's prejudice increased his empathy, helping him to comprehend and empathize with individuals who were equally ostracized. He became a source of comfort and compassion for many who came to the monastery for assistance, particularly the impoverished and outcasts who recognized him as a kindred spirit. Martin's own experiences with discrimination enabled him to connect with them on a deep level, and he found himself particularly qualified to provide relief that went beyond physical recovery. He saw in their eyes the same wounds that had stained his own soul, and his heart ached to soothe them, to assure them of their worth in God's eyes.

Martin's reputation in the community developed as he became more involved with others who were suffering. People described him as a young guy of exceptional gentleness, a healer of both bodies and hearts. The impoverished and oppressed flocked to him, lured not only by his healing abilities but also by the warmth and empathy he showed everyone. He listened to their stories, treated their wounds, and prayed for their healing, exuding compassion that appeared to flow from his very soul. Martin was a unique source of optimism for these people in a world that frequently dismissed them as invisible. He cherished their existence rather than simply tolerated it, seeing in their suffering a reflection of Christ.

Martin felt tremendous satisfaction and a sense of purpose via these acts of service, which masked his own troubles. His compassion for the impoverished and sick became a driving force in his life, a mission that extended beyond his official responsibilities. He began to spend more and more time in the infirmary, tending to the sick with such care that even the friars were impressed. His humble acts of service, which went unrecognized by the rest of the world, provided him with spiritual strength. In these quiet moments of care and compassion, he sensed God's presence more strongly than ever before, a reminder that his life, despite its hardships, was wonderfully blessed.

However, even within the convent walls, Martin felt the sting of rejection. Though he wanted to serve with all his heart, he was acutely aware of the limitations that society imposed on him. He couldn't enjoy the full benefits of the Dominican community, and he wasn't deemed worthy of the title "brother." This subtle exclusion weighed on him, reminding him of the obstacles he faced. But Martin bore this suffering with grace, choosing to see it as a call to greater humility, a road that led him closer to Christ, who had also been rejected and misunderstood.

As Martin went through these tribulations, he grew closer to God, whom he believed had a special plan for him despite the difficulties. Martin emptied out his emotions in the monastery chapel's solitude, expressing his grief and despair via prayer. He prayed for the strength to keep loving, serving, and trusting that God was guiding his life even in the dark. Each prayer was a cry for grace, not just to persevere but also to love those who rejected him, to see in each person a soul loved by God, regardless of how they treated him.

Martin's unwavering faith and humility eventually softened the hearts of people around him, including the friars who had previously despised him.

Many people admired his quiet strength, unwavering eagerness to serve, and compassion for everyone. Even those who had before questioned him learned to respect his character and recognize in him a holiness that transcended societal boundaries. His life, filled with hardships and victories, became a witness to God's ability to transform sorrow into grace.

Martin's spirit was molded in the crucible of difficulty during his early years of tribulation and service, with each act of faith and compassion refining his character. Though the path was steep and difficult, he believed God was guiding him toward something bigger, a purpose beyond his comprehension. Martin grew closer to the life he felt called to lead, one of steadfast devotion to God's will, with each prayer and act of compassion. Martin saw every challenge as a stepping stone, every rejection as an invitation to greater love, as he continued to follow the road God had mapped out for him, guided by faith and sustained by grace.

Embracing Service Over Status

As Martin developed his vocation within the Dominican convent, he realized that his mission extended well beyond simple acts of charity. For him, the road of servanthood was more than just a reaction to discrimination; it was a genuinely conscious decision, a resignation of worldly prestige in favor of a life entirely dedicated to God and others. Martin had felt a tug of humility, an inner desire to live in service and surrender like Christ, since he was a child. This appeal grew louder over time, compelling him to abandon all desires for distinction or recognition and embrace a life that prioritized the needs of others over his own.

Martin's commitment to service was not motivated by a desire to show himself worthy, despite his mixed origins. Rather, it arose from a deep spiritual sense that grandeur rested not in titles or fortune but in unselfish service. Martin believed that the hierarchy of society—based on skin color, family, and wealth—was immaterial in God's eyes. He realized that divine love knows no bounds and that God's kingdom values the downtrodden and humble. For him, this discovery became the foundation of his identity. Martin viewed his labor, no matter how humble, as an opportunity to emulate Christ, who had washed his followers' feet and loved the disadvantaged with similar affection. Martin accepted a type of freedom by giving up the pursuit of personal status, allowing him to devote himself entirely to the service of God's people.

Martin's humility was visible even in the simplest of acts within the monastery's walls. He spent hours doing things that others ignored, like sweeping the floors, scouring pots, managing the gardens, and caring for the animals. No job was too menial, no work was too humiliating, provided it permitted him to serve. His days were filled with tedious and grueling work, but he accomplished each duty with delight and enthusiasm, as if he were doing it for Christ himself. This devotion to the simplest tasks became his kind of worship, a method to return his life to God in a never-ending prayer of appreciation and love.

Martin's reputation for humility grew, and people began to seek him out—not because he held a position of authority but because his presence gave calm and comfort. Those who came to him were often tremendously impacted, not by spectacular actions but by Martin's plain, real kindness. He welcomed the poor, the sick, and the oppressed with wide arms, recognizing them all as treasured children of God. When others were hesitant to reach out to individuals labeled "unclean" or unfit, Martin embraced them with compassion that went beyond social norms. He spent hours in the infirmary, where he not only treated bodily ailments but also provided spiritual solace; his touch was delicate, and his words were few but warm and loving.

Martin's decision to prioritize service over status was not without sacrifice. Even within the monastery, where he was known for his devotion, he was frequently regarded as a mere servant, whose major responsibility was to perform menial tasks. Many of his Christian brothers and sisters couldn't understand his humility or the spiritual riches that his life of service provided. Some misinterpreted his dedication, seeing it as a natural match for someone of his background—a reflection of his "place" rather than a decision. Martin, however, was not bitter. To him, the lack of acknowledgment was a blessing, allowing him to serve without pride or vanity. He felt immense comfort in knowing that his worth was not determined by others' opinions or titles. His identity was based solely on God's love, and this unshakeable basis enabled him to give freely of himself, without regard for praises or recognition.

Martin's decision to live a life of service brought him closer to Christ's teachings, which urged his disciples to be "the least among you." Martin took these words to heart, adopting a spirit of meekness that astounded all who met him. His humility was not performative but truly authentic, stemming from his love for God and desire to show Christ's love in all interactions. He was known not for his sermons or intellectual prowess but for his gentleness, readiness to listen, and deep compassion. To some who saw him, Martin appeared to exemplify radical simplicity, a unique and attractive trait that pushed others to reconsider their own principles.

However, Martin's humility was not passive; it was a purposeful, courageous decision to renounce the dreams that so many others pursued. Martin disregarded the world's expectations by embracing servitude, taking a path that others would have deemed unworthy. Martin stood as a quiet rebuke to a society that valued power, position, and fortune, teaching that true greatness was found in humility and selflessness. He did not strive to rise above others but rather to join them, to stand in solidarity with the oppressed and the marginalized. This decision gave him a unique power, a moral standing that went beyond the formal responsibilities he was allowed to wield. Despite his lack of a title, he had a profound impact on the lives of everyone he met.

Martin's deeds of service went beyond the monastery. Despite his limited resources, he frequently shared what he had with the needy, providing food, clothing, and sometimes money to those in need. He cared for animals with the same love he did for people, seeing a loving God's hand across creation. His affection for animals became another expression of his humility, recognizing that every creation, great or small, was valuable in the eyes of God. In his opinion, there was no distinction between the sacred and the everyday; any act of kindness, whether to a person or an animal, was a means to respect God's creation.

Martin's humble and service-oriented existence gradually transformed the hearts of those around him. His example prompted others to reflect on their own ideals and if their objectives actually coincided with God's purpose. His brethren in the monastery, many of whom had previously looked down on him, were humbled by his unwavering dedication. Though he was never ordained as a priest, Martin's life became a compelling sermon that screamed louder than words could. Through his simple acts of service, he demonstrated the beauty of a life lived for others, one that wanted nothing for itself but offered all out of love.

Martin considered servanthood to be a source of joy rather than a hardship. His heart was filled with thankfulness for the opportunity to serve, to walk in the footsteps of Christ, who had come "not to be served, but to serve." He saw a purpose in his daily chores that went beyond worldly concepts of success and accomplishment. Every hour, whether spent cleaning floors or soothing the sick, became an opportunity to draw closer to God, to give up his own desires in favor of God's. His devotional life was a daily act of praise, a subtle but powerful testimony to Christ's kingdom principles.

As Martin proceeded on this path, he discovered a tranquility that was unaffected by the opinions of others. He understood that his life was a response to God's love, a love that did not require praise or reward. This knowledge allowed him the courage to persevere, even when his humility was misinterpreted or derided. Martin knew in his heart that he was living according to God's will, and that was enough. His life of service became his legacy, a tribute to the power of humility and love, as well as a reminder that genuine grandeur is found in rising others rather than exalting oneself.

Martin's adventure was far from over, and the road ahead would provide problems he could not anticipate. Nonetheless, he walked forth with faith, knowing that God's grace would sustain him through every challenge. His decision to embrace a life of service was both a rejection of the world's ideals and a confirmation of his faith, and it led him to become one of Lima's most revered personalities. Martin discovered a purpose that the world could not provide, peace that the world could not take away, and a joy that only God could bestow.

THE PATH TO HOLINESS

Choosing a Life of Poverty.

Martin de Porres was no stranger to the idea of poverty. He had seen the misery caused by poverty since he was a child—his own family had fought with it, and he had seen how it affected the people of Lima. However, as he matured, Martin saw that poverty was more than simply a condition to be tolerated; it was a way of life that might lead to significant spiritual growth. Martin saw poverty as a means to holiness, a method to match his life more closely with the example of Christ, who chose to live without goods, wealth, or any claim to earthly power.

Martin's faith grew stronger, and he began to feel a strong draw toward the Dominican Order's poverty lifestyle. He was drawn not just to the abandonment of material items but also to the freedom that it brought. Martin knew that by choosing poverty, he could liberate himself from the world's distractions, allowing him to focus solely on his connection with God and service to others. Poverty, in his opinion, was more than just going without; it was about making room for God to fill the void with grace, love, and peace. Martin aspired to most closely follow Christ through this intentional choice of poverty, since he knew Christ had urged his followers to a radical type of discipleship that included self-sacrifice, surrender, and faith in God's provision.

Martin's devotion to poverty was not casual. It was a purposeful, daily decision that influenced his entire way of life. He chose to live without personal goods, relying exclusively on the community and the generosity of others. But this commitment was more than just rejecting earthly prosperity; it was about adopting a worldview of complete reliance on God. Martin's poverty was an act of faith, a refusal to put his reliance in anything but God's divine providence. He lived with a strong feeling of happiness, never seeking more than was required and finding joy in the simplest of ordinary situations. Where others would have seen adversity or lack, Martin saw opportunity: the chance to rely more totally on God, be more compassionate toward the poor, and grow in holiness.

Martin's poverty was characterized by simplicity and joy rather than neglect or misery. He did not give away everything he owned in order to suffer; rather, he gave away everything he had because he had already discovered a higher delight that was beyond goods. His poverty liberated him from the constraints of consumerism, allowing him to live a life of charity, hospitality, and love. It didn't matter how much he had, but rather how he used it. Martin found fulfillment not in acquiring fortune or position but in giving of himself to others, particularly those in need. His dedication to poverty was an outward manifestation of an inner truth: true wealth was measured not in gold or silver but in love, compassion, and a life of service.

Martin's decision to live without personal things was unconventional in a society that valued rank and riches. Poverty was viewed in the Dominican Order as a means of achieving spiritual purity, removing the world's distractions, and allowing one to live more entirely for God. For Martin, spiritual poverty meant more than just giving up luxury; it also meant letting go of all attachment to material possessions. He realized that by doing so, he would be free to live the gospel more fully. His devotion to poverty was not a form of self-deprivation but rather a manner of connecting with God's richness in ways that went beyond worldly possessions. Martin saw every act of giving, whether it was sharing his food, his time, or his love, as an offering to God, a means of acknowledging that all he had originated from the Creator.

Living in poverty drew Martin closer to the poorest of the poor. He had firsthand experience with the hardships of growing up with low resources, and now, as a young man dedicated to poverty, he could connect more profoundly with those who lived in similar circumstances. He saw the impoverished as a community of brothers and sisters in Christ, each deserving of love and respect. Martin did not serve the poor out of obligation; rather, he did so out of genuine love. Martin saw poverty as a lived reality that he shared with those who suffered the greatest. His humble, unassuming existence enabled him to connect with the impoverished in ways that others could not, and it was through this relationship that his holiness thrived.

His commitment to poverty was also deeply spiritual. By living without personal goods, Martin was able to let go of any attachments that might have hampered his spiritual development. He recognized that earthly riches were not intrinsically sinful, but that attachment to them could create a barrier between the soul and God. Martin embraced poverty as a type of detachment—not from the world itself but from the false gods that so frequently seized people's hearts. His poverty was a type of emancipation, a means of surrendering to God's plan free of the constraints of human aspirations.

This dissociation enabled Martin to experience a deeper tranquility that was independent of external conditions. By choosing poverty, he found that true freedom comes not from having more but from wanting less. Martin became a living example of Christ's words, "Blessed are the poor in spirit, for theirs is the kingdom of heaven." His poverty was not only material but also spiritual. He was full of grace, love, and charity, and he generously shared these assets with others around him. For Martin, the kingdom of heaven was not a distant reality but something that could be experienced in the present, in the manner he chose to live his simple and service-oriented life.

Even while he accepted poverty, Martin did not ignore the practical needs of those around him. His profound compassion drove him to care for the ailing, orphaned, and aged. His hands were never idle as he met the spiritual and physical needs of the people of Lima. Martin's life of poverty allowed him to minister in ways that a wealthy life could not, whether by giving the poor food, medication, or a comforting word, or by dispensing the sacraments and prayers. He had no wealth to give, yet he gave everything he had: his time, energy, love, and prayers. His poverty was his greatest gift to those he helped, and by doing so, he fulfilled Christ's charge to love and serve others with a merciful heart.

Many would have perceived Martin's poverty as a life of struggle and suffering. Martin, however, lived a life of peace and joy. He had discovered an abundance in his spiritual life that could not be taken away. His dedication to poverty represented a deep faith in God's provision, and this trust in God's care enabled him to live each day with peace. Martin saw poverty as a way to embrace the whole of God's love and grace, and he embraced it gladly, not to suffer but to become more like Christ, who had nothing but gave everything.

Martin's example eventually inspired countless others to follow in his footsteps. He demonstrated that holiness was not found in wealth or prestige but rather in the desire to give of oneself, to live simply and humbly, and to love others as Christ had loved. Martin saw poverty as a path to holiness, a chance to get closer to God and become the person God had meant him to be. It was a path that led him to a deep, abiding serenity—a tranquility that only people with an attachment-free heart can experience. And in that serenity, Martin discovered a joy beyond comprehension, a joy that would last in the hearts of those he touched for decades to come.

Devotion to the Sick and Needy

Martin de Porres discovered his true calling amid Lima's packed streets, where the impoverished and sick hung out on every corner. He had felt the sting of poverty and discrimination as a young man, but it wasn't until he started working with the underprivileged that he recognized the extent of his calling. The poor, the sick, and the destitute were his people, and he was called to serve them not out of obligation but out of a profound, unwavering love. Martin's devotion to the sick and poor was more than just a charitable deed; it was a ministry, a sacred vocation that he carried out with quiet dignity and compassion.

One of the most outstanding aspects of Martin's work with the impoverished was his ability to see Christ in everyone he saw. Martin treated everyone with the same respect and care, whether it was a beggar on the street, a sick youngster in need of medicine, or an elderly widow who was too frail to care for herself. He recognized that everyone, regardless of class, was God's loving child, and he treated them accordingly. His attitude toward the underprivileged was not arrogant or dismissive; it was one of humility and respect. He saw himself as a servant, not a benefactor or savior, merely carrying out Christ's command to feed the hungry, clothe the naked, and visit the sick.

Martin began his career as a lay brother in the Dominican convent in Lima. Though he held no official position and had no formal medical training, his caring heart and deep faith inspired him to care for the sick and poor in ways that few others could. Every day, he would spend hours caring for the sick in the convent infirmary, comforting them, offering prayers, and administering cures he had learned through years of study and practice. He had a unique ability to cure, whether through prayer, the laying on of hands, or his understanding of herbs and natural treatments. Many of those he cared for were not only physically healed but also spiritually touched by his unwavering faith and kindness.

One commonly reported narrative concerning Martin's healing ministry is of a destitute mother who came to him in despair, her child very ill. The woman had no money to pay for medical care and had seen numerous doctors without success. In despair, she took her infant to Martin, appealing for assistance. Martin didn't hesitate. He held the youngster in his arms, prayed over him, and anointed him with oil. The infant was quickly healed, and the mother, overcome with gratitude, asked Martin how she could repay him. Martin, as he always did, politely declined any recompense, instead pointing her to the one genuine healer: Christ. He told her that God's love was available to anybody who sought it and that she should express gratitude by sharing that love with others.

This anecdote, while exceptional, is not an uncommon incident. Martin's life was filled with similar acts of compassion and charity. He went to the sick's houses, bringing them food, clothing, and prayers. He cared for lepers, a group that was frequently ostracized and secluded by society, providing them with not just physical treatment but also the dignity and respect they so urgently required. His outreach stretched beyond the convent walls to include all of Lima's destitute and disenfranchised. Martin's compassion for the sick and destitute was unbounded, and his dedication to their care was steadfast.

Martin's commitment to aiding the needy, as well as his genuine humility in approaching his vocation, distinguished him from others of his time. He did not seek acknowledgement or praise for his acts of compassion. Instead, he silently went about his task, knowing that his reward would come not from man's plaudits but from God's love. Martin's humility was visible throughout his life. He never boasted about his successes, and he never thought of himself as more important than the people he helped. To him, everyone was equal, deserving of love and respect.

Another outstanding characteristic of Martin's commitment to the sick and poor was his capacity to serve without prejudice. Martin saw beyond the divides of race, class, and social standing that existed in society at the time. He served everyone, regardless of their background or status in life. Martin treated everyone equally with love and care, whether they were Spanish, Indigenous, or African. His determination to break down these barriers and to help people who were frequently disadvantaged and mistreated was a bold act for his day. It demonstrated his strong dedication to the gospel message of love and equality for all people.

Martin, as a lay brother, had a remarkable ability for bringing people together. He inspired the rest of the Dominican community to join him in his efforts to help the needy, motivating them to look beyond their own comfort and reach out to those in need. He was not only a physical healer but also a spiritual healer, conveying Christ's love to the people of Lima via his acts of kindness. His example had a significant impact on those around him, and many of his fellow friars and lay brothers were inspired to emulate his selfless love and service.

Martin stood out not only for his actions but also for his spirit. His presence had a profoundly transformational quality. People who met Martin frequently mentioned the calm and joy that exuded from him, a tranquility that stemmed from his deep connection with God. Martin's service was more than just assisting others; it was about creating a space in which God's love could be felt and experienced in a physical way. When people were in his presence, they knew they were loved and that God was concerned for them. Martin's labor encompassed both physical and spiritual healing, bringing the gospel's promise to a broken and wounded world.

This is illustrated by the story of a guy who had been a lifelong sinner, living a life of drunkenness and greed. He approached Martin in desperation, seeking pardon and guidance. Martin, recognizing the man's repentance, embraced him with wide arms, offering him the love and mercy that he had received from God. Martin prayed with the man, providing him hope and support, and his compassion changed him into a new person. This tale was not exceptional; it demonstrated how Martin's compassion for the sick and poor extended beyond the physical sphere, into the hearts of those he served.

Martin's care for the sick and destitute did not end with his death. Following his death, reports of his compassion and healing circulated throughout Lima and beyond. His reputation as a healer, a helper of the poor, and a man of great faith inspired many. People from all walks of life, rich and poor alike, came to worship Jesus, seeking his intercession and requesting his assistance. Even centuries later, his legacy lives on in the innumerable lives he touched with his compassion for the sick and poor.

Martin discovered his life's true purpose by embracing the destitute and the sick. His love for them was not an afterthought or an obligation; it was at the center of his mission. Through his work, he became a living example of Christ's love for the downtrodden, bearing testimony to the gospel message of mercy, compassion, and hope. His life was a remarkable demonstration of the transformational power of love and service, and his example continues to inspire others who aspire to follow in his footsteps.

Miraculous Moments of Mercy

Martin de Porres' life was defined not only by his great commitment to service but also by an incredible series of supernatural happenings that appeared to stem from his close contact with God. These miracles were not spectacles designed to draw attention to himself but rather quiet manifestations of God's kindness and mercy operating through him. They were moments of divine intervention, when the ordinary became extraordinary, and Martin's humility and love for the poor became the precise conduit through which God's might was revealed. These miracles, witnessed by people around him, verified Martin's sanctity and revealed him to be closely connected to God's heart.

One of Martin's most famous miracles was his ability to heal the ill in ways that defied natural explanation. Stories about his miraculous healings circulated swiftly around Lima, and many people came to him for relief from maladies that doctors couldn't treat. What distinguished Martin's healing touch was not just the bodily repair but also the profound tranquility and spiritual rebirth that came with it. When patients came to Martin for healing, they often departed feeling not just physically better but also spiritually invigorated, with a fresh sense of faith and hope.

There was a story of a young girl who had been suffering from a severe fever for weeks. Her parents had tried everything, and nothing seemed to work. Desperate, they took her to Martin. Martin immediately laid his hands on the kid and prayed for her. At that point, the fever broke, and the girl regained her vigor. The parents were overwhelmed with gratitude and asked Martin what they could do in back. Martin simply smiled and encouraged them to thank God, as God's power, not his own, had healed the boy.

This story is not a unique instance. Martin's healing abilities expanded to a wide range of illnesses, from fevers and infections to more puzzling and complex conditions. His great faith in God enabled him to approach each case with trust, believing that the cure would be brought about by God's will rather than his own. He never claimed credit or praise for the miracles that happened through him. He was continuously pointing back to God, telling people he healed that the power they observed was a result of God's mercy and love, not his own righteousness.

One particularly moving miracle involves a woman who had been crippled for many years. She had given up hope, thinking that her condition was irreversible. When she learned of Martin's healing ministry, she went to the convent where he lived, determined to ask for his prayers. When she approached, Martin took her hands in his and silently prayed for her healing. As Martin prayed, the woman felt a sense of warmth and serenity, and then she began to experience weird sensations in her limbs. Her body gradually responded, as if prompted by an invisible power. She rose up, taking her first timid steps in years. She went on her knees, overcome with emotion, and thanked God for her amazing cure.

Martin's supernatural power was witnessed by the clergy and his fellow Dominican brothers, as well as the impoverished and sick. One such occurrence occurred when a fellow friar became seriously ill with a fever that left him unconscious for days. When Martin learned of his brother's illness, he hastened to the sickroom right away, carrying with him some herbs and oil he had prepared. As he prayed over the friar, the fever broke, and the brother awakened fully restored. Those who witnessed this miracle were astounded not only by the sick man's recovery but also by the profound serenity and tranquility that enveloped the room as Martin prayed. It was as if God's presence had descended on them, immersing them in grace.

Martin's healing abilities extended beyond bodily problems. He had a rare ability to soothe troubled minds and alleviate spiritual suffering. Many who came to him seeking not just physical healing but also spiritual advice discovered that his simple and humble remarks contained deep knowledge that calmed their concerns and doubts. His capacity to listen, console, and utter words of peace was as remarkable as his ability to heal the ill. Those who sought his advice left with feelings of calm and confidence, knowing that God had answered their prayers through the intercession of his servant.

Martin's capacity to multiply food was one of the most astounding of his supernatural powers. It is reported that when there was a lack of provisions at the convent or a large number of people arrived seeking food, Martin would pray over the limited supplies they had, and the food would multiply to feed everyone. On one occasion, the nuns were in the process of preparing a basic lunch when word spread that a big crowd of destitute people had gathered outside, hungry and in need. The friars were concerned about feeding everyone with such a limited supply of bread and veggies. Seeing their predicament, Martin gently took the food, prayed over it, and distributed it. Fortunately, there was enough to feed the entire company, with plenty leftover. This was not the first time such a miracle had occurred, and it further added to the growing consensus about Martin's sanctity.

Perhaps one of Martin's most stunning miracles involves the animals under his care. Martin had a strong affinity with animals, particularly the stray dogs, cats, and rats that roamed the convent grounds. His love for all of God's creatures was clear in the way he handled them: with respect, sensitivity, and concern. When the convent was overrun with rats, Martin calmly prayed for them to leave. To everyone's surprise, the rats departed, leaving the monastery clean of the infestation. His compassion extended to all living beings, and his extraordinary capacity to care for God's creation became a symbol of his deep connection with all of creation.

Despite the numerous miracles credited to Martin, he never sought popularity or recognition. He lived in continual humility, deflecting praise and directing others to God. He understood that these miracles were not about him but about the power of God's compassion and mercy at work in the world. In his heart, he was only a vessel, a conduit for divine grace through which God's kindness flowed.

Even after his death, the miracles persisted. Many people claimed receiving miraculous healings and having their prayers answered via Martin's intervention. His reputation as a miracle worker developed, and Pope John XXIII canonized him in 1962, recognizing the extraordinary life he had led—a life distinguished not merely by deep humility and service but also by the obvious presence of God in everything he accomplished. Martin's miracles were indications of God's kingdom coming into the world, demonstrating that God's mercy and love were available to anyone, particularly the poor, sick, and disenfranchised.

Martin was not at the heart of any of these remarkable experiences. Rather, the focus was on God's love flowing through him. The miracles were performed for God's glory rather than his own. They demonstrated Martin's close relationship with his Creator and exposed to the world God's limitless compassion and mercy, which Martin embodied in every act of his life.

Transforming Lives through Compassion

Martin de Porres' unusual life had an impact not just on people around him but also on the heart of Lima. His compassion, born of a profound and genuine love for God, changed the lives of many people, lifting them from the depths of despair to a place of hope and healing. These stories, full of genuine gratitude, demonstrated the power of love and compassion—the sort of love that crosses boundaries, heals scars, and shines light into the darkest of places.

One of the most striking elements of Martin's ministry was his capacity to see the humanity in everyone he met, regardless of social rank or circumstance. Martin broke down societal barriers of race, class, and ethnicity with an open heart and a soft touch. His love knew no boundaries. His legacy of compassion was actually developed via his caring for the sick, impoverished, and outcast.

There is a moving story of a woman named Maria who suffered immensely from an illness that left her bedridden and frail. Her family had spent a significant amount of money seeking medical attention, but their efforts were futile. Maria's family, in desperate need, learned of Martin's healing abilities and chose to take her to the monastery. When they arrived, they were greeted with the simplicity of Martin's heart rather than the promise of miracles. He welcomed them with open arms and took the time to hear their story. Martin prayed for Maria, but more importantly, he remained by her side, offering words of encouragement and hope. Maria's life was transformed not just by the healing touch but also by the profound sense of being recognized and cared for during her time of need. Maria eventually regained her health, but it was Martin's love for her, not the miracle itself, that she would remember for the rest of her life.

Then there was the story of Felipe, a little boy living on Lima's streets. Felipe, who was orphaned at a young age and left to fend for himself, had become accustomed to living in isolation, striving to survive in a world that seemed unconcerned about his existence. One frigid winter evening, he was walking the streets looking for something to eat when he came into Martin. Rather than passing him by, Martin stopped and encouraged Felipe to accompany him to the convent, where he could receive warmth, food, and rest. Felipe was initially apprehensive, having previously experienced rejection from others, but something in Martin's eyes—something that spoke of care and understanding—convinced him. Martin provided Felipe with more than just food and shelter; he gave him dignity. For the first time in his life, Felipe felt valued because of his kindness and compassion. Felipe found not just physical sustenance under Martin's care but also emotional support, which he had long been without. Martin's compassion alleviated more than just his hunger; it also restored his sense of worth.

The Dominican friars' testimony was as essential, as they regarded Martin as a living example of the truths they preached. The friars would frequently watch Martin spend hours in prayer and service to others, never seeking recognition and always directing gratitude to God. One friar related that Martin once spent the entire night caring for a sick guy who had no relatives to help him. Despite his exhaustion, Martin did not hesitate to offer his assistance. He remained by the man's side till morning, offering comfort and prayer. The monk marveled at Martin's compassion, which appeared to flow from an inexhaustible reservoir supplied not by human strength but by divine love.

Martin's kindness extended to the animals he cared for at the convent. Martin was frequently seen by the Dominican friars tending to the stray dogs and cats that roamed the grounds, feeding them and treating their wounds. His affection for these creatures was deep, and there were numerous cases where animals that had been hurt or unwell were healed while under his care. He regarded all creatures, human and animal, with the same care and reverence. One friar related an incident in which Martin treated a wounded dog that had been brought to him. He treated the dog's wounds, and within a few days, it was completely healed. The friar observed that Martin's act of compassion was not only a miracle in and of itself, but it also demonstrated the depth of his love for God's creation.

Martin's love had a transformational effect that extended beyond those who were physically healed or comforted. His kindness had a significant impact on the spiritual lives of everyone he met. Martin provided renewed hope to many people who had become disillusioned or weary of their faith. His sweet demeanor and simple faith shone like a beacon in the darkness, drawing others back to God's love. A woman named Isabel, who had been suffering with spiritual issues, recalls meeting Martin. She had initially thought of him as simply another friar, but there was something about him that stood out. She noted how when she spoke with Martin, he listened to her concerns and uncertainties without passing judgment. He didn't give her huge theoretical solutions; instead, he simply revealed his own deep love for God and how it nourished him in all situations. His genuineness and tranquility left a lasting impression on Isabel, and their chats helped her rediscover the joy of her faith.

Martin's unwavering compassion touched even the hardest of hearts. Thomas, a former thief who had lived a life of crime and immorality, approached Martin for forgiveness. He was burdened with remorse and shame, as if there was no turning back from his past. However, when he met Martin, his heart underwent a profound transformation. Martin did not judge Tomas for his past; rather, he welcomed him with open arms, reminding him of God's limitless kindness. Tomas was extremely moved by Martin's love and forgiveness, and with Martin's help, he was able to quit his life of crime and devote himself to serving others.

All of these instances demonstrated that Martin's compassion was a reflection of God's love acting through him rather than an act of charity. His love was not a passing feeling but a continual and unrelenting energy that tried to lift up the broken, the lost, and the suffering. It was love that transformed people's physical, emotional, and spiritual existence. This metamorphosis was marked not only by Martin's amazing feats but also by the profound peace, hope, and dignity he restored to those who encountered him. Martin demonstrated to others that the ultimate power of compassion comes not in spectacular displays but in quiet, everyday acts of love that touch the deepest corners of the heart.

THE HEART OF A HEALER

Healing Hands, Divine Gifts

Martin de Porres was already well-known as a healer before his canonization. His name was whispered with reverence not only in Lima but across Peru. His ability to heal—whether it was a fevered body, a sick spirit, or a shattered community—was not simply a product of his commitment but also a divine gift flowing from the depths of his relationship with God. Healing, for Martin, was more than just a job or a charitable deed; it was a manifestation of Christ's compassion, a divine calling marked by a special grace.

His healing ministry began with humility. It began with calm, compassionate acts of service rather than grandiose shows of supernatural power. His patients were frequently individuals that others had abandoned—the impoverished, the sick, and the ostracized. They were not only physically hurting but also spiritually devastated. Martin saw their pain as a doorway to the divine, and through his actions of care and kindness, God's love was made apparent.

The early healings that were recognized in Lima were simple but effective.

Martin would visit the sick and, with a delicate touch, console them with his prayers. Divine mercy would present itself in the midst of his ministry when no one was looking and no one expected a miracle. People began to talk about his gift, and the rumors swiftly spread throughout the city. They would come in droves, suffering from illness, starvation, and despair, seeking out the Dominican lay brother who appeared to hold God's love in his own hands.

A woman named Clara told a story that exemplified Martin's early healing ministry. Clara had been bedridden for several months due to a terrible sickness. Her family sought the greatest medical therapy possible, but all efforts were useless. In a final attempt to treat her, they took her to the convent where Martin lived. When Martin arrived, he did not provide her the normal medicines or therapies of the day but rather gently placed his hands on her and prayed. His words were simple, yet his faith remained firm. Clara, though feeble and in considerable pain, felt a peculiar peace wash over her. The next morning, to the surprise of her family, she awakened entirely recovered. This was not the outcome of any earthly treatment, but rather the work of God through Martin's hands.

However, Martin did not see these healings as a chance for personal fame or glory. He never claimed credit for the marvels that happened around him. Those who observed these healing works remarked on Martin's tendency to deflect acclaim, constantly pointing to God as the ultimate source of his strength. His humility in the face of such supernatural events distinguished him from other figures of the day. For Martin, healing was always about giving honor to God, not making a reputation for himself.

However, the divine essence of his healing gifts was more than just bodily restoration; it was also about the overall transformation of the person. Martin's healing ministry emphasized the soul and spirit just as much as the physical body. People who came to him were generally looking for both bodily and spiritual healing. Martin knew this profoundly. He understood that most of human pain was spiritual rather than physical. Physical illnesses were frequently a manifestation of spiritual scars. Thus, every healing was accompanied with prayer, a listening ear, and Christ's profound love. Martin believed that simply healing the body was insufficient; he tried to heal the person as a whole, providing peace to the soul while comforting and relieving the body.

One of the most powerful parts of Martin's healing ministry was his capacity to heal simply by being present. Often, his profound, sympathetic gaze and quiet words had the biggest influence on those he ministered to, rather than the laying on of hands. It was as if, by his basic acts of caring, he was welcoming people into a space where they may feel God's love in its most pure form. One man, bedridden and alone, described how Martin came to see him. He had given up hope due to his sorrow. However, when Martin entered the room, he felt a sensation of calm flood over him. Martin's sheer presence appeared to carry the presence of God, and the man's anxiety and suffering began to decrease. It seemed as if the presence of Christ Himself had entered the room.

Beyond physical healings, Martin's miracles were frequently spiritual in origin. In one prominent case, a little girl with a serious emotional wound came to Martin for comfort. She had been rejected by her family because of her mental illness, and she had begun to feel hopeless. Martin spent hours with her, listening to her anguish and then delivering a prayer of intercession before speaking encouraging words that changed her life. The girl, previously burdened by the weight of her misery, found peace in her heart and was reunited with her family. It was a spiritual healing rather than a physical one, and it served as a tremendous testimony to Martin's ability to minister in all aspects of life.

Of course, the miraculous healings that occurred in Martin's presence did not only affect humans. His concern extended even to the animals under his care. Many reports describe Martin curing ailing animals, feeding stray dogs, and tending to the injured. This reflected his sense of the interdependence of all creation. In his opinion, there was no distinction between the sacred and secular, human and animal. Every aspect of creation, in some way, expressed God's love. As a result, just as Martin cared for the people of Lima, he also showed compassion to all creatures in need.

One particularly memorable anecdote is that of a sick puppy abandoned by its owners. The dog, weak and near death, was brought to Martin's convent. When Martin saw the animal, he instantly took it in his arms and treated it with the same care and compassion as he would a human person. He treated the dog's wounds, fed it, and prayed for it. The dog was eventually restored to health, and its owners, who had no idea where it was, were surprised when it returned to them, totally recovered. This was also a sign of the heavenly work that Martin did every day, an evidence of God's love in a world that frequently disregarded the most vulnerable.

Martin's miracles were not the conclusion of the story; rather, they marked the beginning of a deeper truth: healing is always a labor of divine mercy. It is beyond our control, and it cannot be described by human logic. True healing comes from God alone. Martin knew this better than anybody else, which explains why his healing ministry was so effective. It was never about him, but about God's love flowing through him to others.

Martin's healing restored not only bodies but also people's relationships with God. His work as a healer was a physical manifestation of God's mercy and love, a love that transcends all suffering and returns us to the Father. Martin's legacy as a healer is not only about the miracles he performed but also about how he inspired others to experience God's healing love. It was this love that transformed Lima and still inspires people today.

Faith in the Midst of Suffering

In the middle of his suffering, Martin de Porres' life showed a vital truth: real healing is not only the absence of pain but the ability to bear it. Martin's faith was genuinely tested in the midst of human pain, in the eyes of the sick, the poor, and the brokenhearted. His ability to connect with individuals in sorrow stemmed not from ordinary sympathy but from a profound understanding of God's presence in the midst of suffering. He was more than just a witness to human suffering; he became one with those who faced it, walking with them as a servant of God.

Martin's empathy for others stems from his own personal sorrow as a young man. His mixed-race origins as the son of a Spanish lord and a liberated African slave placed him in a social limbo. He was not entirely accepted by the European elite or totally welcomed by indigenous and African groups. This seclusion throughout his adolescence taught him firsthand what it means to be ignored, misunderstood, and rejected. He knew what it was like to be rejected because of one's background rather than their acts or character. This early experience with sorrow would serve as the foundation for his subsequent empathy for others.

Martin's bodily agony was also a recurrent feature of his trip. Though he was famed for his incredible healing talents, he, too, suffered from chronic disease and physical suffering throughout his life. In fact, it was not uncommon for him to be ill for extended periods of time, yet he never let this stop him from helping others in need. The man who healed others in amazing ways was also stricken with disease, yet he bore it with grace and unshakeable faith in God. His faith was not affected by personal sorrow; rather, it grew stronger, becoming a source of support for others.

One of Martin's most noticeable characteristics was his unwavering reliance on prayer, especially during times of adversity. When confronted with his own sorrow, whether bodily or mental, Martin placed total trust in God. He did not try to avoid or complain about his discomfort. Instead, he used it to get closer to God, offering his pain as a type of solidarity with Christ's suffering. His deep personal life of prayer became the foundation of his ministry, allowing him to serve with compassion and humility, even in the face of his own shortcomings.

One illustration of Martin's faith in the face of adversity happened after an outbreak of disease that swept across Lima. Many people in the city had died as a result of a severe fever, and hospitals were overrun with patients. Despite his own precarious health, Martin quickly offered to help with the care of the sick. He did not hesitate, despite the risk of infection and the exhaustion he was certainly experiencing. His heart was moved with compassion for those who were suffering, and his faith gave him the strength to persevere. His efforts were driven by a strong confidence in God's ability to use his own flaws for His purposes, rather than a need for acclaim. Many who were on the verge of death were restored, not just literally but also spiritually, as they felt God's love through Martin's hands.

However, Martin's empathy was not only visible in his healing ministry but also in the quiet moments of sorrow he experienced privately. His time in the infirmary, where he spent hours caring for his own infirmities, was one of intense prayer and thought. His solitude became a place where his faith matured. Martin would pray to God in the silence, seeking comfort in His presence. He would frequently pray for the strength to persevere, asking God to utilize his suffering for the benefit of others. And in such moments, his faith became a witness to everyone who saw him. Despite his own suffering, he stayed constant in his love for God and people around him.

Martin's confidence in suffering was further demonstrated when he served as a lay brother in the Dominican Order. Despite having no official medical background, he was frequently called upon to assist with patient care. As he walked from person to person, catering to their needs, he would frequently pray for them. He had a special knack for understanding the actual causes of their suffering—whether physical, mental, or spiritual—and ministered to them accordingly. Martin realized that healing was more than just mending the body; it was also about nurturing the spirit. Many of the sick were not only healed but also left with a great sense of inner peace as a result of his prayers and kindness.

Martin discovered the genuine meaning of kindness during these difficult times. His empathy was not motivated by pity but by a true comprehension of the human experience. He saw that pain, when combined with Christ's own passion, becomes a source of grace. Martin frequently described hardship as an opportunity to join in Christ's redemptive work. He felt that with prayer and faith, any grief or sadness could be converted into something holy. This notion was not academic for him; he lived it every day. When he observed someone in pain, he didn't just say words of comfort. He prayed for them with intensity and zeal, inspired by his own pain.

Many of the sick who came to Martin for healing experienced not just physical healing but also spiritual regeneration. They were moved not only by the mending of their bodies but also by the deep serenity emanating from Martin's soul. His empathy was contagious, leading others into God's presence, where they, too, could find healing. This was the defining feature of Martin's ministry: it was never about the miracles themselves, but rather what they spoke to—God's enormous love for each individual, regardless of their state of suffering.

Martin's healing gift is claimed to have affected not only humans and animals but also the natural world surrounding him. When the region's crops were threatened by pestilence, Martin would frequently pray over them, asking God to spare them. His prayers were not only answered but also yielded copious harvests. He recognized that all of creation was intertwined with God's love and that suffering in one region of the world might be alleviated by prayer, faith, and God's mercy.

Martin's empathy for the suffering was more than an emotional reaction to sorrow; it was a reflection of his confidence in God's destiny. He was profoundly convinced that God had a plan for each person's suffering and that by bearing it with faith, one could bring about divine transformation. His own suffering became a means of uniting with Christ and participating in the world's redemption. Through his life, Martin demonstrated that faith in the midst of suffering is not only feasible but also the route to holiness. Through his suffering, he was able to touch the lives of many individuals, bringing them healing, peace, and hope for salvation.

Martin demonstrated to the world that healing entails more than just alleviating physical ailments. True healing occurs when we release our pain to God and allow His love to transform it. Martin saw every moment of suffering—his own or others'—as an opportunity to grow in holiness and experience God's redemptive love.

Miraculous Cures and Encounters

Saint Martin de Porres' life was defined by an astonishing succession of miraculous healings and encounters that not only demonstrated the depth of his spiritual connection with God but also highlighted his tremendous compassion for the suffering of others. These miracles, while sometimes small and inconspicuous, were powerful manifestations of divine grace operating through a humble and dedicated servant of God. They were not miracles for the sake of spectacle, but acts of kindness and love that transformed lives, gave hope to the hopeless, and demonstrated God's power working through a man who had spent his entire life helping others.

One of the earliest and most well-known reports of Martin's miraculous cure involved a young girl suffering from a particularly virulent fever. She had been suffering for days, her family despondent and unable to afford the medical care she required. When word spread about Martin's capacity to heal, the girl's relatives, in desperation, brought her to the convent where he worked. Martin, noted for his humility and refusal to accept credit for any cure, did not execute elaborate ceremonies or boast about his own ability. Instead, he just prayed for her, softly resting his hands on her forehead, and asked God to cure her in accordance with His plan.

The next day, to the surprise of her family and neighborhood, the girl awakened entirely recovered. Her fever had subsided, and her strength was completely restored. It was the direct effect of God's kindness, as asked by Martin's prayer, rather than any human action. The news of this miraculous treatment traveled fast around Lima, and many people seeking healing sought out the modest friar. Martin's approach to healing was always based on prayer, and he believed that restoration came via God's mercy rather than his own strength. His prayers were infused with a deep trust that God would respond according to His will, and it was in this submission that the miracles flowed.

There were countless other accounts of miraculous cures, some well-documented and some whispered in Lima's streets. One such case was a woman who was paralyzed from the waist down. She'd spent years confined to a bed, unable to walk, and in chronic discomfort. Her health appeared bleak, and she had almost lost faith in the chance of recovery. Desperate and eager to try everything, she went to Martin, who was known for his ability to cure such ailments. Martin kneeled alongside her, praying for God's aid. He prayed frantically, resting his hands on her legs and imploring God for the strength to heal her. To the surprise of everyone there, the woman suddenly regained movement in her legs. She sprang from her bed, her paralysis completely gone, as if it had never occurred.

These miraculous healings were not limited to the human body but also affected animals and the natural world. Martin had a strong affinity for animals, especially those who were frequently mistreated or neglected. He was known to care for stray dogs, cats, and even farm animals, exhibiting a deep love and respect for all of God's creations. It is believed that when Martin prayed over animals, they would become unusually quiet or heal from disease. One of the most moving anecdotes is about how he treated an ill dog that had been abandoned by its owner. The dog had suffered horrific injuries and was left to die. Martin, noting the creature's distress, took it into his care and began nursing it back to health. Within days, the dog had not only been healed but also found a loving home with one of the friars, who adopted it as their own pet.

Martin's supernatural gifts extended to the plants and produce. When the region's harvests were threatened by drought or pestilence, people flocked to Martin for prayers. He would go into the fields and diligently beg for rain or protection against the harmful pests. Several times, the skies opened up, providing much-needed rain to the area. The crops would prosper, and the people would be amazed by the seeming power of Martin's prayers. These signs were more than just evidence of his ability to alter nature; they were manifestations of God's compassion and kindness in a world that frequently appeared oblivious to human need.

Martin's miracles were not limited to physical healing. He also possessed a unique ability to discern the spiritual needs of those who came to him. Many people came for physical recovery, but others sought Martin's advice for emotional or spiritual issues. They, too, discovered healing in his presence. One man had long battled with rage and bitterness in his heart. He had been involved in a violent altercation and had gone to Martin seeking not only physical recovery but also spiritual serenity. Martin prayed with the man, using his trademark compassion, asking God to cleanse his heart of the bitterness and wrath that had devoured him. The man left Martin's presence with a great sense of serenity, his heart free of the load of anger. It was a miracle of the soul, not the body—an act of kindness that proved Martin's insight that true healing transcends bodily restoration; it is the mending of the heart and spirit that transforms lives.

There were also amazing interactions with people who desperately needed God's grace, such as convicts and social outcasts. One particularly heart-breaking interaction occurred with a thief who had been apprehended and brought to the friary in shackles. The man, hardened by years of crime, was expected to exhibit no remorse. But when he got in touch with Martin, something unexpected happened. The thief was moved by Martin's generosity and gentle nature, and he burst into tears, admitting his offenses and pleading for forgiveness. Martin is supposed to have forgiven the man and provided him a route to atonement in a peaceful, meditative manner. The interaction revolutionized the thief's life, inspiring him to abandon his criminal existence in favor of a new life based on religion. This was another miracle, although one of spiritual rebirth and transformation, which was possibly the most deep of them.

While many of these miracles were witnessed by the people of Lima, Martin's humility meant that he never claimed credit for them. He would frequently credit the cures and miracles to God's mercy, deflecting praise away from himself and constantly pointing to the source of the power: God. Even in the middle of incredible circumstances, Martin maintained his composure, never allowing the miraculous nature of his deeds to inflate his ego or drive him to seek praise. His priority was always to serve God and His people.

The reports of Martin's miraculous cures and encounters make it obvious that his talents were intended to convey God's mercy and love rather than to highlight his own glory. Martin became a living vessel of God's mercy thanks to his humble acts of prayer, desire to serve the sick and needy, and strong faith. His miracles were not random acts of marvel but rather manifestations of God's tremendous love for the world, working through a man prepared to spend his life completely in obedience to His plan.

Martin's miracles continue to inspire people today, reminding us that true healing, whether physical, emotional, or spiritual, comes from God and is provided by those who, like Martin, choose to live lives of selfless service, strong faith, and compassionate love. His contacts with others in need of help serve as an example of what it means to be a faithful servant of God, expressing Christ's healing power in every moment.

The Gift of Inner Peace.

While Saint Martin de Porres' miracles were often impressive in their physical nature—curing diseases, restoring shattered bodies, and even healing animals—his approach to healing was based on a deeper, more fundamental gift: peace of heart. Martin saw that genuine healing entailed not only the restoration of bodily health but also the healing of the spirit and the provision of serenity that transcended the worries of this world. In a world full of sorrow, anguish, and uncertainty, Martin recognized that peace—God's peace—was the ultimate treatment, a gift that could alter not only a person's body but also their spirit.

This gift of inner serenity was arguably most represented by Martin's response to other people's anguish and suffering. Rather than focusing exclusively on the surface symptoms, he saw that long-term recovery starts with a deep inner peace. For Martin, peace was a heavenly gift that he needed to acquire from God before he could give it to others. His prayer life, which was characterized by great dedication and persistent surrender to God's will, enabled him to serve as a conduit for this serenity. And it was this tranquility that distinguished Martin as a healer—not just for his miraculous cures but also for his capacity to soothe the hearts and minds of people who came to him in anguish.

One of the most important parts of Martin's therapeutic method was his capacity to bring comfort to persons in emotional or spiritual distress. Many people came to him seeking tranquility in the middle of personal problems, rather than a solution for physical ailments. Anxious, depressed, or grieving people frequently found comfort and hope in Martin. He was not just a physical healer but also a spiritual healer, offering a safe haven for individuals who felt lost in their sorrow.

There was the case of a woman who had been in severe grief following the death of her small child. Her anguish had overwhelmed her, leaving her heartbroken and unable to find comfort. She came to Martin, unsure what to expect but hoping for some sort of comfort. Martin, with his quiet and loving demeanor, listened to her narrative without judgment, allowing her to weep. But more than that, he gave her the gift of tranquility. After hearing her grief, he prayed over her, asking God to ease her agony and offer peace to her shattered heart. The tranquility she felt in that moment was remarkable. She didn't leave with an instant solution to her sadness, but she did leave with a deep sense of peace, knowing she wasn't alone and that God's love surrounded her in her pain.

This inner serenity was not limited to those who were in mourning or in distress. It extended to anybody who came into contact with Martin, for his entire existence was a live example of Christ's peace. Even individuals who attended with physical illnesses frequently left with a greater sense of peace than when they arrived. This was not to suggest that Martin overlooked their bodily needs; rather, he recognized that true recovery necessitated a holistic approach that included not only the body but also the soul.

In reality, many of the people Martin physically healed also experienced significant spiritual healing as a result of his ministry, which brought them into a deeper connection with God. They discovered not only bodily alleviation but also an internal metamorphosis that enabled them to live more contentedly. Martin's approach to healing always emphasized God as the ultimate source of peace. He never claimed credit for the miracles that occurred through him, instead attributing them totally to God's favor. For Martin, healing was never about personal glory or notoriety; it was about being an instrument of God's love and peace.

One particularly affecting story of how Martin's peace of mind affected others includes a guy who came to him for treatment from a physical illness that had afflicted him for years. The man had tried everything, including visiting doctors and exploring other ways of healing, but nothing had worked. His body had weakened, and his spirit had grown tired from the protracted pain. When he first met Martin, he was looking for a quick fix, anticipating a miracle cure to relieve his physical suffering. However, as he spent time with Martin, something changed inside him. Martin, rather than focusing exclusively on the physical condition, inquired about his life, relationship with God, and spiritual well-being. The man came up about his issues with faith and his ongoing concern about his future.

Martin, with his typical humility and gentle insight, did not provide an immediate solution. Instead, he prayed with the man, asking for peace in his heart and the courage to give his anxieties to God. Over time, the man's health began to change, as did his view on life. His body recovered gradually, but more importantly, his spirit was restored. He discovered peace by trusting God and letting go of his incessant anxieties. The genuine miracle of that day was not just the physical recovery but also the peace.

Martin's deep spiritual connection to God was the source of his inner tranquility. His personal life was defined by humility, simplicity, and steadfast faith in God's providence, which helped him stay grounded in the face of adversity. He did not seek achievement, recognition, or financial prosperity. Instead, he accepted poverty and humility as ways to draw closer to God and serve His people. This great faith in God's purpose for his life gave him a peace that was visible to everyone who met him.

In his ministry, Martin frequently spoke of peace as a heavenly gift available to those who sought it with an open heart. He frequently reminded individuals he healed to give their problems to God and believe in His divine will. He understood that tranquility could not be found in material riches or successes but rather in the silent surrender of one's heart to God. This teaching was more than just theoretical; it was reflected in Martin's daily behavior. His life demonstrated that true serenity comes from an inner confidence in God rather than external conditions.

Martin's legacy as a healer is inextricably linked with the gift of inner serenity he gave to those in need. His miracles were more than just physical healings;

they were spiritual transformations that allowed people to experience God's peace in the midst of pain. He taught that true healing necessitates not only physical repair but also emotional tranquility, which can only be obtained by a close relationship with God.

As we reflect on Martin's life and work, we are reminded that God wants to offer each of us the gift of peace. In a world that is frequently overwhelmed by chaos and suffering, Martin's life serves as a poignant reminder that God's peace is always available to us if we are prepared to open our hearts to it. Just as Martin was a vessel of God's peace at the moment, we are also asked to be instruments of peace in our own lives, giving healing and consolation to people around us via the peace that God has entrusted to us.

ENDURING TRIALS WITH FAITH

Bearing the Cross of Prejudice

Martin de Porres was born carrying the weight of a culture that did not completely welcome him. Martin was born in Lima, Peru, to a Spanish aristocrat and a liberated African lady, and his mixed heritage distinguished him in a culture divided by rigid social hierarchies. His father, a nobleman, abandoned the family shortly after his birth, leaving his mother to raise him in poverty. Despite the noble blood in his veins, Martin would never be fully accepted by the highest echelons of society, nor by the entire African or indigenous groups. Martin's natural duality—half European, part African—meant that he had to carry the cross of prejudice and exclusion his whole life, but he did it with extraordinary grace, perseverance, and unshakeable faith.

The social structure in 16th-century Peru was profoundly divided by race. Spanish colonists, who wielded power and wealth, looked down on indigenous people and African slaves, thinking them inferior. This sense of racial superiority pervaded practically every facet of society, from the church to the marketplace, the workplace to the family. People of mixed ethnicity, like

Martin, were frequently marginalized, denied opportunities, and considered second-class citizens. These preconceptions would have been agonizing for anyone, but for Martin, who was born into a society of discrimination, they were the harsh reality of everyday life.

Martin first felt the pain of rejection because of his appearance and ethnicity when he was a child. Children from noble families, with their pale skin and privileged status, teased him for his darker color. Though Martin's Spanish father was a high-ranking official, his abandonment of Martin and his mother meant that the youngster would never completely acquire the benefits of his heritage. Martin's mother, a freed African woman, was also frequently looked down upon, and this stigma remained with him throughout his life.

Despite the hostility he encountered, Martin's heart was not hardened by resentment. Instead, he looked to God for strength, and it was through his faith that he was able to face the harsh realities of racism. His meek acceptance of his social situation was motivated by a genuine faith in God's divine design, not resignation. Martin saw his hardships, including persecution and hostility in his own community, as opportunities to grow closer to Christ. In his sorrow, he perceived an opportunity to follow in the footsteps of Jesus, who, like him, was rejected and reviled by people He came to serve. Martin's capacity to withstand these challenges with patience and grace demonstrated his deep faith and dedication to God.

Martin entered the Dominican Order at the age of 24 and found it to be a valuable source of shelter. Even within the order, Martin encountered difficulties. Though he was accepted by the brothers, his mixed ethnicity and poor upbringing put him in a lower social standing than many of his fellow friars. As a lay brother, Martin did mundane jobs like cooking, cleaning, and caring for the sick, which many others in the Order thought were beneath them. Nonetheless, Martin approached his activities with enthusiasm and humility. Rather than seeking higher position or notoriety, Martin found joy in serving others, thinking that his ultimate calling was to be a conduit of

God's love and mercy, even in the most simple and overlooked ways.

Even inside the order, Martin's mixed origin was not overlooked. Some of the more wealthy Dominican Order members, who came from wealthier backgrounds, made disparaging remarks about his appearance and racial heritage. Martin was subjected to whispers and scornful eyes, but he refused to be discouraged. Instead, he continued to lead a life of prayer, kindness, and humility. His steadfast faith and commitment to assisting others enabled him to climb beyond Lima's socioeconomic divisions.

Martin's personal relationship with God was the foundation that kept him going through these challenges. He found peace in prayer and meditation, using these times of spiritual intimacy to gain strength and guidance. He realized that the cross he bore—marked by racial prejudice and social marginalization—was not his alone. He believed that Jesus, who had suffered immensely for the benefit of humanity, was sharing his agony. This idea allowed him the resolve to face the derision of others, knowing that his suffering served a purpose beyond human comprehension. Martin's life was a great example of how to bear the cross of prejudice and discrimination with dignity and grace, constantly looking to Christ as the ultimate model of perseverance and love.

Martin's capacity to forgive those who tormented him because of his color was another impressive aspect of his personality. He never carried grudges, even against those who treated him cruelly. His heart was devoid of bitterness, and he consistently decided to respond to hatred with love. He knew that in order to heal and improve the world, one must first love those who appear difficult to love. This act of forgiveness was a profound expression of his understanding of the gospel, in which Christ emphasized forgiveness as a basic element of the Christian life. Martin understood that by forgiving others, he was following Christ's example and accepting the divine grace that God freely extends to all.

One of the most remarkable parts of Martin's life was his ability to see past the racial divides that existed in his society. He was discriminated against because of his mixed race, yet he never let it define him. Instead, Martin concentrated on what brought him together with others—his shared humanity and faith in Christ. Martin's compassion went across race and class. He cared for all individuals, rich or poor, noble or enslaved, regardless of their social standing or origin. He considered everyone a loving child of God, deserving of dignity and respect. This spirit of inclusivity and love was central to his healing ministry, which impacted countless lives and inspired many others to see past superficial differences and embrace the Gospel message of love and unity.

Martin's mixed origin and the prejudices of his period posed significant hurdles. Martin, however, was able to overcome these obstacles thanks to his strong faith, deep love for God, and dedication to helping others. His life is a striking example of how faith can help us overcome seemingly insurmountable challenges and how, in the face of discrimination, we may choose to respond with compassion, grace, and forgiveness. In doing so, we bear not just our personal crosses but also serve as instruments of healing and reconciliation in a broken world.

Faith in the Flames of Adversity

Martin de Porres was challenged in ways that would have broken many people's spirits, yet his faith remained unshaken, and his perseverance in the face of hardship demonstrated his deep, unwavering trust in God's providence. Born into a world where his entire existence was viewed as a contradiction—an illegitimate child of mixed race—Martin could have easily succumbed to the trials and injustices that surrounded him. Instead, he handled each adversity with great tenacity, gaining strength not from his surroundings but from the unwavering power of his faith.

One of Martin's most impressive characteristics was his ability to face adversity without losing his sense of calm. While his life was filled with adversity—personal rejection, cultural derision, and even bodily pain—he stayed steadfastly committed to God. Martin had challenges that many would consider insurmountable beginning in his childhood. His mixed heritage put him in a vulnerable social position, denying him the rights enjoyed by others at the time. Rather than retreating into bitterness, Martin chose to accept his circumstances, viewing them as possibilities for spiritual growth.

Martin encountered new challenges when he became a lay brother in the Dominican Order. His lowly origins limited his ability to participate fully in the fraternity. He was frequently assigned menial tasks such as helping the sick and impoverished, cleaning, cooking, and caring for animals, which were considered beneath the more affluent members of the Order. Martin, nevertheless, accepted these obligations with great devotion. The menial labor he did was not a burden for him but rather a way to draw closer to Christ, who had also humbled Himself in service to others. He found joy not in recognition but in carrying out God's desire in all actions, no matter how small.

Martin's resilience was also displayed by his reaction to the hostility he faced. Though his fellow Dominicans and Lima residents often looked down on him because of his color and class, he never let others' malice define him. In a society where racism was prevalent, Martin may have easily absorbed his rejection, allowing it to undermine his sense of self-worth. Instead, he regarded discrimination as an opportunity to carry Christ's cross. He never responded in rage or self-pity, but rather with the same patience and love that Jesus showed during His own suffering. His capacity to face such adversity without resentment was a striking testament to faith's transformational power.

Martin's response to bodily pain provided the most striking demonstration of his perseverance. Martin's body was fragile, and he had bouts of ill health all his life. Instead of surrendering to the suffering, he surrendered it to God out of love and devotion. Martin's determination to endure suffering without complaint demonstrated not only his strong faith but also his profound love for Christ. He understood that suffering, when combined with Christ's passion, might be used to participate in the world's redemption.

Several examples from Martin's life demonstrate his exceptional ability to bear adversity while maintaining his enthusiasm and faith. One of the best-known stories is about how he was assigned to caring for a poor, ailing woman whom everyone else had abandoned. The woman was in the last stages of a terrible illness and was not expected to live long. Despite the severe circumstances, Martin demonstrated amazing compassion by sitting with her day and night, responding to her needs, and praying for her recovery. His love for this woman was so strong that he not only provided bodily care but also consoled her spirit with words of hope and encouragement. The woman, who had lost faith in mankind, was extremely moved by Martin's charity, and it was stated that his love and prayers brought her calm and miraculous healing. This anecdote is a fantastic example of Martin's capacity to find faith in the face of adversity. He saw suffering not as something to be avoided but as an opportunity to love and serve others in Christ's name.

During his struggles, Martin resorted to prayer for strength. He spent several hours in the chapel, seeking God's presence and guidance. Martin's prayer life was profound and intimate, and it was through prayer that he found the tranquility and perseverance required to face adversity. He saw prayer as more than just a ritual, but as a connection to God, a source of power and nutrition for the spirit. His devout commitment not only helped him get through difficult times, but it also served as a powerful witness to people around him. People frequently commented that there was something special about Martin's prayer life—something that exuded sanctity and drew others to seek him out for advice, counsel, and consolation.

Martin's relationship with God was the foundation of his perseverance. He never saw his trials as something to dread or avoid, but rather as an opportunity to strengthen his faith in God's purpose for his life. In the face of rejection, poverty, and pain, Martin remained firm, believing that God was with him at all times. His reaction to hardship was one of hope, anchored in God's love and the notion that, through faith, all things are possible.

Furthermore, Martin's perseverance was more than just an internal strength; it had an impact on people around him. His fellow friars and the people of Lima were moved by his unshakeable faith and selfless service. They saw in him a real example of how God's grace can transform even the most challenging circumstances. Martin's actions demonstrated that true strength comes not from the absence of misfortune but from the ability to face it with love and trust.

Martin's story is a strong reminder that religion is more than just professing a belief; it is actually tested and developed in the crucible of struggle. Martin's faith, like gold purified in fire, became stronger with each struggle, and it was during these tribulations that his holiness shone the brightest. His unwavering determination in the face of discrimination, misery, and tragedy serves as a tremendous message for all of us. Faith, when established in God, can weather any storm, and in the midst of hardship, it can emerge stronger.

As we reflect on Martin's response to his life's hardships, we are reminded that our own trials, while unpleasant, are opportunities to enhance our relationship with God. Just like Martin trusted in God's plan for him, we must also believe that our challenges have value and purpose in God's broader plan. And, like Martin, we are supposed to not only endure but also embrace our crosses with faith, tenacity, and love, knowing that God would never abandon us in the midst of suffering.

The Power of Forgiveness

One of the most fundamental features of Martin de Porres' life was his constant devotion to forgiveness, which distinguished him as a living example of Christ's teachings on mercy. In a world full of injustice, bigotry, and cruelty, Martin's reaction to wrongdoing was diametrically opposed to what society may have anticipated. Where others might have nursed resentment, sought vengeance, or carried grudges, Martin chose the road of mercy, forgiving even those who had mistreated him severely.

Martin had every reason to be resentful from a young age. Born into a society in which persons of mixed race and low beginnings were frequently looked down on, he could have easily internalized the prejudice and discrimination that characterized his life. Instead of allowing these injustices to define him, Martin chose to rise above them, using one of the most powerful tools available: forgiveness. He saw that forgiveness was not just a means of restoring relationships but also a powerful tool for liberating one's soul from the bonds of bitterness and anger.

One of the most stunning examples of Martin's forgiveness came during his time at the Dominican monastery in Lima. Martin was extremely committed to helping his community and carrying out his duties, yet he encountered significant hostility from some of his fellow friars. As a lay brother, he was viewed as lesser to the Order's ordained members, and he was frequently subjected to severe treatment by others who saw him as less deserving. Some would insult his mixed ethnicity, while others would assign him the dirtiest, most degrading tasks, claiming that they were appropriate for someone of his origin. Despite this, Martin never expressed bitterness or rage. Rather than responding with cruelty, he provided love and service in exchange. He treated those who belittled him with the same care and tenderness that he offered to Lima's poorest and most marginalized residents.

Martin's ability to forgive was not based on human power but rather on a deep spiritual conviction that forgiveness was central to the Christian message. He was inspired by Christ's example, who, while nailed to the cross, requested God to forgive His persecutors: "Father, forgive them, for they know not what they do" (Luke 23:34). Martin realized that in order to fully follow Christ, one must forgive not only those who beg for it but also those who feel no guilt and may never seek forgiveness. He saw forgiveness as a radical act of love, with the potential to heal wounds and bring peace where there was conflict.

In one particularly painful event, Martin was wronged by a Dominican Order member. This brother, envious of Martin's spiritual skills and the respect he had acquired from the people of Lima, began spreading false tales about him. He accused Martin of things he didn't commit and attempted to damage his reputation. Most individuals would have been justified in confronting the brother or seeking vengeance, but Martin's reaction was nothing short of extraordinary. Rather than defending himself or retaliating, he decided to pray for his accuser. He said nothing negative about the sibling, and when others brought the unfairness to his attention, Martin just replied, "I forgive him." He requested God to forgive and bless the man, despite the fact that he had been harmed.

This act of forgiveness was more than just a passive acceptance of wrongdoing; it was a forceful assertion that Martin's peace of mind and spiritual integrity did not depend on the approval or condemnation of others. He chose instead to put his trust in God's justice. His forgiveness was not an attempt to disregard the wrongs done to him, but rather to let go of the need for retaliation and enable God to bring true justice. Martin proved the ability of forgiveness to stop the cycle of anger and hurt, replacing it with peace, love, and reconciliation.

Martin's forgiveness was much more extensive in his outreach to the impoverished and sick. He frequently encountered people who had been treated unfairly, ranging from beggars and criminals to those who were socially excluded. Many of these persons had been abandoned by their families or communities, either due to prior transgressions or their social rank. Nonetheless, Martin never hesitated to express compassion to them. His forgiveness was not confined to forgiving those who had harmed him individually but also included global compassion for everyone who had been wronged by society.

One particular anecdote jumps out: Martin was caring for a man who had been severely damaged in a tragic accident. The man was very humiliated by his appearance and believed that no one would love him because of his scars. Others had avoided him, seeing him as less than human because of his appearance. But Martin saw past the surface. He saw a soul in need of healing—not just physically but also emotionally and spiritually. Martin offered him forgiveness, not only for how he had been treated by others but also for whatever resentment he had toward those who had harmed him. He helped the guy heal by demonstrating that the power of forgiveness could restore more than just physical health—it could also restore dignity, hope, and peace of mind.

Forgiveness was also fundamental to Martin's connection with God. In his own prayers, he frequently pleaded for forgiveness, not only for his own mistakes but also for those of others. He saw that forgiveness was a two-way street. To forgive others, one must be willing to seek and receive forgiveness from God. Martin accepted in humility that no one is sinless and that forgiveness and healing can only be obtained through God's kindness.

Martin's forgiveness was witnessed by many people throughout his life, and it became one of his distinguishing features. Martin's example frequently transformed angry, bitter, and resentful people. His forgiveness was more than a gesture; it was a profound act of grace that brought about healing, restoration, and reconciliation in the lives of those who received it. Martin's ability to forgive transformed him into a channel of God's grace in a culture that frequently chooses retaliation over healing. His life demonstrates that forgiveness is a source of strength and spiritual force rather than a sign of weakness. By forgiving, we liberate ourselves from the bonds of anger and bitterness, allowing God's love to flow through us and transform both ourselves and the world around us.

For Martin, forgiveness was more than a passive act; it was a way of life, one he practiced on a daily basis, even in the face of personal betrayal and injustice. His example challenges us all to go past our hurts and complaints and take the radical road of mercy. As Christ forgave those who persecuted Him, so are we invited to forgive, not merely in words but also in deed, for it is through forgiveness that we truly represent Christ's heart and contribute to the healing of the world.

Perseverance in Prayer

For Saint Martin de Porres, prayer was more than just a ritual or a way to find peace in difficult times; it was the fundamental cornerstone of his life. In a world filled with discrimination, hardship, and personal challenges, his constant devotion to prayer proved to be the secret to his resiliency. Prayer provided him with strength in the face of hardship, inner calm in the midst of upheaval, and a means of deepening his relationship with God.

Martin's mother instilled in him the value of prayer from a young age. Growing up in a poor and religious environment, he learned the importance of connecting with God via quiet periods of thought and prayer. Martin's understanding of prayer, however, grew deeper as he developed. For Martin, prayer was more than just reciting words or doing prescribed rituals; it was a continuous conversation with God that fed his spirit and carried him through the most difficult times of his life.

Martin remained committed to prayer despite the trials he endured, including societal discrimination, the difficulties of living as a lay brother in a cloistered order, and a terrible sense of isolation from his father. His life was characterized by an incredible level of devotion that went beyond the formal prayers made in the chapel. Martin would frequently escape to a secluded area, away from the distractions of the world, to spend lengthy hours in prayer. In these moments, he sought not just spiritual assistance or intercession but also to hear God's voice, believing that in solitude he would discover the wisdom and tranquility he so desperately needed.

Martin's prayer life was marked by both simplicity and passion. He did not try to impress others with eloquent lectures or lengthy liturgies; rather, he sought the Lord in the silence of his heart. His prayers were deep, genuine, and heartfelt. He frequently used his humble surroundings to reflect on God. Whether working in the infirmary or doing menial jobs at the monastery,

Martin would discreetly offer up his efforts as a form of worship. He considered everything in his life as an offering to God, and every moment was an opportunity to praise and converse with the divine.

His perseverance in prayer was especially obvious during times of extreme pain. Throughout his ministry, Martin experienced numerous personal obstacles. He was frequently subjected to prejudice, contempt, and discrimination as a result of his mixed origin. Nonetheless, his prayer habit provided him with the fortitude to persevere during these difficult times. In the stillness of his prayers, Martin found solace. Prayer gave him the courage to forgive those who harmed him, as well as the strength to continue loving those who rejected him. Prayer became a safe haven for his heart, providing healing and repair.

Martin's approach to spiritual trials, when the weight of his battles appeared insurmountable, was always the same: prayer. He realized that the difficulties he was facing were not a sign of God's desertion but rather an invitation to grow closer to Him. Martin saw prayer as a way to relinquish his will and believe in God's divine purpose. He believed that by praying, God would give him the strength to persevere and the intelligence to see the lessons concealed in his suffering.

One of the most striking elements of Martin's prayer life was the depth of his inner tranquility. Despite his outward troubles, he exuded a calm that perplexed many around him. His fellow friars and those who sought his assistance frequently commented on his calm temperament, even in the face of the most severe circumstances. Martin indicated that the serenity he felt came from his everyday conversations with God. In prayer, he gained the courage to face each day with tranquility, knowing that God was always present, guiding him and giving him the strength to persist.

Martin's prayer life was not an escape from reality but rather an engagement with the world. His prayers were rooted in the realities of his daily existence, responding to the needs he saw around him. Martin's prayer was more than a passive ritual as he cared for the ill, the destitute, and the disenfranchised; it was a driving force that fuelled his service to others. Through his frequent prayers, he sought to connect his will with God's, transforming himself into an instrument of divine mercy and compassion. His intimate contact with God enabled him to provide compassion and care to those in most need, and prayer provided him with the strength to persevere through the emotional and physical strain of his work.

One story demonstrates Martin's devotion to prayer. Martin is supposed to have spent hours in the chapel, kneeling before the Blessed Sacrament, asking for direction and strength. One evening, while praying, he felt a strong feeling of God's presence, and he was overwhelmed with profound calm. His battles with racial prejudice, feelings of solitude, and the weight of his responsibilities were all lifted in that moment of heavenly connection. This period of tranquility did not mean that Martin's problems vanished, but rather that he was able to confront them with fresh vigor and a stronger sense of purpose.

As Martin's reputation developed, individuals from many walks of life approached him for help, seeking both physical healing and spiritual comfort. During these encounters, Martin would frequently pause to pray for his visitors, asking God to give them the strength to face their own hardships and the faith to believe in God's love. His prayers were not just for his own well-being but also for the benefit of others. He interceded for the sick, the afflicted, and the oppressed, believing that God's kindness would flow through him to provide healing and peace.

Martin's constancy in prayer served as an example for many who followed him. His unshakable faith in God, even under the most difficult circumstances, was a strong testament to the transformative power of prayer. He knew that God was with him at all times, whether he was at peace or going through a difficult time. Martin's prayer was not a single act but rather a social gift that connected him to the broader body of Christ, and it was this constant contact with the divine that gave him the courage to endure.

Finally, Martin's life serves as a reminder that prayer is more than just asking for things; it is also about developing a close relationship with God. This bond gives us the courage to overcome adversity and transform the world around us. Martin's life is a call to all of us to persevere in prayer, to believe in God's plan, and to let His love sustain us through every adversity.

THE MIRACLES AND MYSTERIES OF ST. MARTIN

Visions and Spiritual Encounters

Saint Martin de Porres' life was impacted not just by acts of compassion, service, and healing but also by mystical experiences and visions that revealed his profound spiritual connection with God. These meetings, some of which were witnessed by others, revealed a man who was connected to the divine in ways that went beyond ordinary human comprehension. His spiritual experiences were more than just personal revelations; they deepened his faith, strengthened his commitment, and fueled his desire to help the impoverished and suffering.

Martin's mysticism did not involve big shows or spectacular public displays. Instead, it was distinguished by a peaceful, humble relationship to the divine that was frequently felt in solitude or when completing mundane duties. Martin saw these visions not just for his own benefit but also as heavenly messages to guide his service to others.

One of the most well-known reports of Martin's mystical encounters came during his prayer sessions. During these profound moments of connection with God, he frequently had visions of Christ, the Virgin Mary, and other saints. These highly personal meetings have been described as moments of profound tranquility and enlightenment. During one such vision, Martin is reported to have received a supernatural message encouraging him to continue his work with the poor and downtrodden. The vision reminded him of his earthly mission: to serve those in most need, as Christ had done.

Martin's visions were deeply spiritual but also profoundly practical. Martin once had a vision of the Blessed Virgin Mary, who told him about his work with the sick. She encouraged him not to give up, even when his efforts appeared futile, and comforted him that his acts of charity were known to God. This vision encouraged Martin to persevere amid difficult times, reminding him that his job was in accordance with God's intention. For Martin, such visions were not transient occurrences; they were affirmations of his divine mission and reminders that his little efforts were part of a larger divine plan.

Another account claims Martin had a vision of Saint Dominic, the founder of the Dominican Order to which he belonged. Saint Dominic appeared to him at a time when Martin was questioning his vocation and dealing with difficulties as a lay brother. Saint Dominic encouraged Martin to continue his efforts, assuring him that his humility and dedication were acceptable to God. This vision marked a watershed moment in Martin's life, providing him with not only the confirmation he needed but also the spiritual counsel he needed to keep on track.

One of the most striking characteristics of Martin's visions was his humility in receiving them. He did not seek out spiritual experiences in order to elevate his personal standing. Instead, he saw them as gifts that demonstrated his dedication to a life of service and humility. He frequently kept his spiritual encounters private, only discussing them with those closest to him, and he never attempted to make them the major center of his ministry. Martin saw the miracle not in the vision itself, but in how it boosted his faith and allowed him to continue his work.

Martin's visions were not limited to moments of prayer only. It is reported that he had divine encounters while performing his daily chores. Whether tending for the sick, feeding the destitute, or cleaning the convent, Martin would occasionally be seen in intense concentration, as if communicating with someone invisible. Those around him would occasionally hear him talk gently, as if conversing with angels or saints. On one occasion, a fellow friar saw Martin kneeling in the yard, his face gleaming with an inner light, as if he were encircled by a divine presence. The friar, who had known Martin for many years, later stated that he had never seen anyone with such a calm and bright expression.

Perhaps the most notable aspect of Martin's mystical existence is his ability to levitate while praying. Witnesses reported that while Martin was in serious prayer, his body would rise off the ground and hang in the air as if caught in a supernatural embrace. Martin never sought this phenomenon; rather, he saw it as a proof of his intimate relationship with God. Those who observed it were frequently moved to tears, seeing this remarkable incident as a visible affirmation of Martin's sanctity and commitment.

Martin's visions were not always comforting and encouraging. He also faced great spiritual trials, including periods of darkness and desolation. Martin apparently felt distanced from God during these moments, which the mystical tradition refers to as the "dark night of the soul." Martin's faith was put to the ultimate test during this time. Even in these times of spiritual dryness, Martin remained strong in his dedication. He continued to pray, serve, and believe in God's plan even when he didn't feel God's presence. These periods of adversity enhanced his humility and understanding that faith is not necessarily based on emotional experiences but rather on trust in God's will, even when it appears concealed.

Saint Martin's mystical encounters had a transformational effect on both him and those around him. People who witnessed his visions frequently mentioned the calm and sanctity that exuded from him. His spiritual encounters seemed to imbue his activities with divine purpose, and those who received his care—whether physical treatment or spiritual guidance—left feeling touched by the divine. Martin's ministry was both spiritual and practical. His visions did not separate him from the world but rather grounded him in it, allowing him to serve others with elegance and strength that changed lives.

One of the most important aspects of Martin's mystical existence was his ability to transcend the limitations of his time. His experiences with the divine were not limited to the rich or powerful. He recognized saints, angels, and Christ Himself in the poor and oppressed people he served. This supernatural insight in the faces of outcasts became the defining feature of his ministry. His mystical experiences were about more than simply personal contacts with the divine; they were also about seeing the sacred in all humans, particularly the most vulnerable.

Saint Martin of Porres' visions and spiritual encounters are more than just historical accounts; they invite all believers to pursue a deeper, more intimate connection with God. Martin's example reminds us that the divine is always present, whether in prayer, service, or pain. His life demonstrates that holiness is more than just miraculous occurrences; it is a daily commitment to helping others with love and humility, led by a vision of God's presence in everything.

Miracles of Multiplication and Provision.

Saint Martin de Porres' miracles were more than just acts of spiritual healing and divine comfort; they were also signs of God's abundant sustenance. One of Martin's most amazing miracles was the multiplication of food and resources, which helped the hungry, poor, and needy. These miraculous interventions demonstrated not just Martin's close relationship with God but also His inexhaustible love for society's most vulnerable people.

Many people came to the convent for food, shelter, and care in Lima, a bustling metropolis plagued by poverty and inequality. Martin, who had dedicated his life to helping the underprivileged, frequently found himself with few resources. Despite the scarcity of food, he always believed that God would provide. And in many cases, he was proven correct.

One of the most well-known miracles of multiplication took place when a big gathering of hungry people arrived at the convent. The convent's kitchens were small, and the food supply was almost gone. Martin, unfazed, requested that the food be served. When the cook reported that there was insufficient food for everyone, Martin reassured him that God would supply. As he prayed over the limited supplies, a remarkable event occurred: the food began to expand, enough to satisfy all of the guests and leave some leftovers. Those present observed this miracle and were astounded by the wealth that arose from so little. It was a clear indication to everyone that Martin's confidence in God's provision had been recognized in the most visible and exceptional way.

On another occasion, Martin was caring for a huge number of destitute and ailing people, some of whom had traveled from remote districts of Lima. The convent's food supply was running dangerously low, with little possibility of getting more before the next delivery. Undaunted, Martin took the remaining food and began distributing it, silently praying as he went. Despite the large number of individuals who showed up, the food never appeared to run out. As each person received their piece, it became clear that there was significantly more food available than had been previously anticipated. According to some reports, baskets containing bread, fruit, and other provisions were replenished as soon as they were empty. Witnesses to the miracle were emotionally moved, and many were inspired by Martin's persistent faith in God's providence.

Food was not always multiplied in response to a pressing necessity. Martin sometimes accomplished these miracles out of pure love for mankind and a desire to help. A group of hungry orphans from the local orphanage once visited the nuns after a long day. Martin, noting their plight, dispatched his helpers to gather whatever food was available. But when they returned, they discovered that the pantry was empty. Martin remained undeterred, smiling and praying over the empty shelves, begging God to deliver. As they watched, the shelves began to fill with bread and food from virtually nowhere. The children were fed, and the pantry remained full, demonstrating the limitless source of God's love when one pushes ahead in trust.

One of the most moving examples of supernatural providence occurred when Martin came across an impoverished family in desperate need of assistance. The family has no food to eat and no way of getting it. In their despair, they approached Martin for help. After hearing their dilemma, Martin requested they wait while he went to his room to pray. He returned empty-handed. However, as he entered their poor home, the family was surprised to see a basket of bread and other food in front of their door. The miracle, while small, was profoundly meaningful. For the family, it symbolized God's personal concern for their suffering. For Martin, it was a reminder of the power of prayer and the significance of believing in God's capacity to meet His people's needs.

Martin's miracles showed a deeper reality about God's wealth of spiritual gifts, in addition to multiplying physical resources. These miraculous provisions were frequently accompanied by moments of serious meditation and prayer, during which Martin gently reminded people around him that true food was often spiritual rather than material. After observing the multiplication of food, Martin assembled the crowd and spoke to them about the significance of receiving Christ in the Eucharist. He emphasized that, just as God provided for their physical need, He also provided for their spiritual hunger by feeding them with the Bread of Life. This experience, like so many others, demonstrated Martin's deep connection between physical and spiritual nutrition, a connection that transcended worldly borders and pointed to God's eternal love.

Martin's multiplication miracles were genuinely extraordinary in their ability to transcend material scarcity and become signs of hope for those in greatest need. In a world when hunger and poverty were commonplace, Martin's deeds of heavenly provision showed that God had not forgotten the needy. His miracles were not spectacular or flamboyant; they were quiet, humble acts of love performed with the sole purpose of relieving the suffering of others. Martin's acts of multiplication, whether feeding a group of sick patients, a family in need, or a mob of hungry youngsters, spoke to the essence of his mission: to serve, to love, and to believe in God's limitless ability to supply.

Martin's miracles of multiplication and provision were intended to display God's generosity as well as to meet immediate physical necessities. They were a reminder that God's love knows no bounds and that His care extends to everyone, no matter how small or insignificant they appear in the sight of the world. Martin's miracles revealed that even in the most difficult situations, God's love is always present, overflowing, and ready to overflow.

These stories of supernatural provision spread not just because of the remarkable character of the events but also because they highlighted Martin's lifelong compassion and humility. His determination to help others, regardless of the personal cost, and his unshakeable faith in God's provision were central to his sanctity. Martin de Porres' miracles made him a living witness to the wealth of God's love and mercy, and his legacy continues to inspire others who strive to live generous, compassionate, and faith-filled lives.

Breaking the Laws of Nature

Saint Martin de Porres is remembered not only for his profound deeds of generosity and service but also for remarkable miracles that defied natural law. These incidents were more than just manifestations of heavenly power; they also demonstrated Martin's unshakeable faith, intimate relationship with God, and ability to transcend the boundaries of human comprehension. His life was filled with inexplicable incidents that astounded everyone around him and served as a poignant reminder that God's reach stretches far beyond the limits of nature and human reason.

The account of miraculous people and item transportation is one of Martin's most well-known miracles. Martin, in his humility, had no lofty goals or wishes to gain attention to himself, but he became famous for accomplishing things that astounded those who watched them. Several versions describe how Martin, when there appeared to be no other way to help others, used his talent of miraculous transportation to defy time and space, carrying objects across distances in minutes.

In one case, a guy requested Martin's assistance with an urgent need—he needed to send an essential letter across town, but the roads were congested and transportation was slow. Martin, sensing the gravity of the situation, volunteered his assistance, despite the fact that it appeared impossible. To the surprise of the guy and others, Martin prayed over the letter, and in an instant, the letter was transported to its designated destination, with no visible means of transportation. The observers were speechless, unsure how such an occurrence could have occurred. While the world was restricted by the constraints of time and distance, Martin's faith enabled him to overcome those limitations in a miraculous fashion, serving as a living reminder of God's limitless power.

On another occasion, Martin was asked for assistance in the middle of the night. An impoverished family had grown ill, and no one else could care for them. The roads were hazardous, and Martin would have been unable to reach them in time. Nonetheless, in what many characterize as a moment of heavenly grace, Martin knelt to pray, trusting in God's will. When he awoke, he was already at the family's door, having covered the long distance in the blink of an eye. His deep faith in God enabled him to overcome all natural obstacles—distance, time, and circumstance—and fulfill the call to serve.

However, Martin's miracles extended beyond the movement of people and objects. There were countless reports that his prayers appeared to change the path of nature itself. One particularly dramatic story occurred during a strong storm. The Dominican monastery where Martin lived had just received a shipment of crucial supplies, but the ship was stranded in the storm, and its cargo was in danger of being lost at sea. The storm was so fierce that there appeared to be no chance for the crew or their cargo. The anxious convent members gathered to pray, and Martin, moved by compassion for those at sea, participated in the intercession. As he prayed, the storm unexpectedly subsided. The winds eased down, the skies parted, and the ship arrived safely in port with its cargo intact. The storm that had earlier appeared impenetrable was suddenly gone, as if nature had reacted to the pleas of one humble servant of God.

In addition to these amazing happenings, Martin was recognized for having a special rapport with animals, which further blurred the borders between nature and the supernatural. He exhibited tremendous empathy for all living beings, and his interactions with the animal realm frequently resulted in amazing events. He was said to be able to speak with animals and even soothe violent or wild ones. On one occasion, a gang of stray dogs had been wreaking havoc in the region, and the villagers were angry by their behavior and wished to drive them away. Martin, upon hearing this, approached the dogs and spoke to them calmly. The dogs quickly stopped their disruptive behavior, leaving many villagers in awe, asking how he did it. What appeared to be an everyday interaction was actually tremendous evidence of Martin's deep harmony with God's creation.

Perhaps one of Martin's most spectacular miracles occurred when he was summoned to save a man who had become critically ill. The man, suffering from a severe fever, was unable to travel to the monastery, and his family had already given up hope. They contacted Martin, who, upon hearing the plea, quietly prayed in his tiny cell. A few seconds later, the sick man appeared at the convent's door, having walked despite his serious condition. When questioned about how he made the trek, the man said he felt a sudden rush of strength, as if someone had lifted and carried him. Though natural laws would have suggested that he was too ill to walk, it was apparent that supernatural intervention had overcome all physical constraints, and Martin's prayers healed the man.

Another of Martin's unusual incidents was the miraculous quenching of a fire. A massive fire had broken out in the convent's kitchen, and despite repeated attempts to suppress it, the flames became dangerously out of control. The smoke was so heavy that the air became almost unbreathable. Martin, who happened to be nearby, ran to the scene out of desperation. Rather than using physical tools to extinguish the fire, he simply prayed aloud for God's intervention. As soon as he concluded his prayer, the flames vanished, as if they never existed. The witnesses were stunned, unable to understand how the fire had been quenched so quickly and wonderfully.

These events, which defied the natural rules of time, space, and the elements, were not purely coincidental. Each of them was founded on Martin's unwavering faith and relationship with God. Martin was a man who understood that God is the Creator of the universe and hence has authority over all aspects of creation, both natural and supernatural. Martin was able to tap a force that the human mind cannot fully comprehend, allowing him to be an instrument of divine intervention in ways that astounded and inspired others around him.

Each of these amazing incidents conveys a clear message: faith, humility, and confidence in God can conquer even the most overwhelming obstacles. For Martin, these miracles were not meant to bring him glory but to draw others to God's greater glory. His miracles, while remarkable, were always an extension of his service to others, a visible manifestation of his tremendous compassion for the impoverished, sick, and suffering. They were an invitation to those who witnessed them to look beyond the visible world and place their trust in the Creator's unlimited kindness and omnipotence.

Martin's violation of natural laws serves as a constant reminder that, in God's perspective, no obstacle is too large, no constraint is too fixed. For those who walk with faith, anything is possible. His life and miracles continue to inspire others who strive to follow Christ, demonstrating that through humility and prayer, the divine can interact with the ordinary in ways that change people's lives forever.

A Living Witness of Divine Love

Saint Martin of Porres' life was a powerful example of divine love in action. His miracles, acts of generosity, and humble service were not isolated incidents; they were the result of a heart completely devoted to God's purpose and a soul thoroughly tuned into Christ's love. Martin's life demonstrates that divine love is not remote but rather present and active in the world through those who are prepared to serve and give of themselves.

Martin demonstrated a love that went beyond human understanding from his early years in Lima. His mixed-race parentage put him at a disadvantage in society, but he harbored no animosity or anger. Instead, he welcomed God's love, knowing it was inclusive and all-encompassing. This heavenly love inspired Martin to help those who were often forgotten by society—the poor, the sick, the imprisoned, and the ostracized. Martin became a living conduit of God's unlimited compassion, providing a glimpse into God's heart via his simple yet profound acts of mercy.

One of the most striking ways Martin expressed divine love was through his healing ministry. The miracles that flowed from his hands were more than just exhibitions of supernatural power; they also demonstrated God's great concern for the suffering. Martin's healing abilities were not performed for personal glory, nor were they viewed as a source of power over others. Rather, these were acts of love—God's love shown in the lives of individuals in severe need. Each miracle was an answer to someone's grief or need, a divine intervention that revealed God's loving presence in the most intimate and personal manner.

Martin believed that love was more than just spectacular gestures and public accolades. His had a gentle, often unrecognized love for service. Whether he was cleaning the infirmary, feeding the impoverished, or caring for the sick, his efforts were motivated by a strong conviction that every deed, no matter how simple, had everlasting meaning. He recognized Christ in everyone he met, and his love for others reflected his love for Christ. Martin's life became a mirror, reflecting God's love to a world in need, demonstrating that true love is not about recognition or position but about devoting oneself entirely to the service of others, as Christ did.

The miracles Martin accomplished were the result of his intimate oneness with God, but they also allowed God to show His love for all of creation. Many people's lives were changed as a result of these miraculous events. The ill were healed, the impoverished were fed, and the outcasts were accepted. Beyond these tangible acts of charity, Martin's life extended a more profound invitation: to believe in the transformative power of divine love. His miracles served as a reminder that no one is beyond God's reach, that God's love is limitless, and that with faith and prayer, even the most difficult situations may be redeemed.

One of the most moving illustrations of Martin's function as a living testimony to divine love came from his interactions with animals. He treated all of creation with great respect and care, seeing in each thing a reflection of God's love. One of the most memorable stories of his benevolence involves the animals in his community. When the friars complained about the rodents in the kitchen, Martin asked them to depart in the name of God. Not only did the rats go, but Martin's capacity to speak with the animals became a powerful symbol of God's compassion for all living creatures, both human and animal. His acts of charity extended even to individuals who were considered pests or nuisances by the rest of the world, demonstrating that divine love knows no bounds.

Martin's life also demonstrated the power of forgiveness. In a society where people typically hold grudges and seek vengeance, Martin chose the higher road of love and healing. Even when faced with intense prejudice, discrimination, and derision because of his ethnicity and status, Martin never became angry or bitter. Instead, he chose to forgive those who had harmed him and love them as Christ had loved him. His willingness to forgive, even when offended, is one of the most obvious signs of his love for God and humanity. Martin's forgiveness did more than just restore relationships; it was a living testament to God's unlimited love, which forgives all faults and extends grace to those who seek it.

Throughout his life, Martin's love was accompanied by prayer. His strong prayer practice was more than just a personal devotion; it was the foundation for everything he achieved. His love for God inspired his love for others, and his prayers became an offering of love to God on behalf of everyone in need. Martin saw that his love for others was not his own; it came from God's endless wellspring of grace. His humble and surrendered prayers were a way for him to continually align his heart with God's plan and, as a result, allow God's love to flow through him and to others.

One of the most striking elements of Martin's life was that his love was free of expectations and restrictions. Unlike many who seek attention for their good deeds, Martin's love was freely offered without the desire for acknowledgement. He served with delight, a gracious heart, and a deep sense that every act of service, no matter how tiny, was eternally valuable. Martin demonstrated throughout his life that love is about giving rather than receiving. He gave himself totally, providing everything he had—his time, energy, prayers, and ultimately his life—as a living testimony of God's unlimited love.

Saint Martin's life was not only a reflection of divine love but also an encouragement to others to live loving and service-oriented lives. He demonstrated that God's love is a living reality that may be experienced through everyday acts of mercy, kindness, and selflessness. His example encourages us all to go past the surface and perceive the divine in every person, act of service, and moment of love.

Looking back on Martin's life, we are reminded that love is the best of all qualities. It is the foundation of all God's operations in the world, and it is the most valuable gift we can give to others. Martin de Porres demonstrates that love is more than simply an emotion; it is a choice to serve, forgive, give without expectation, and live with an open heart to God's purpose. His life demonstrated the transformative power of love, and it is through this love that we might become living witnesses to God's unlimited mercy.

LEGACY OF LOVE AND MERCY

A Heart for All Creation

Saint Martin de Porres is best known for his deep love and compassion for humanity, but his heart went far beyond humans. One of the most notable elements of his sanctity was his profound and reverent concern for all of God's creation, particularly animals. To Martin, the natural world was more than just a backdrop for human life; it was a reflection of God's glory and a member of the heavenly family that he was compelled to serve and defend. His sensitivity to animal needs, his unique connection to nature, and his recognition of all creatures as integral parts of God's rich and beautiful creation were all important aspects of his spiritual journey and legacy.

Martin had a special bond with animals from a young age. As a boy growing up in Lima, he was known for caring for stray animals and being kind to everyone he encountered. Whether it was a stray puppy, a sick bird, or the rodents in the friary kitchens, Martin's attitude toward the animals was always compassionate. This relationship to nature was more than a fascination; it was an extension of his spirituality, proving that his love for God extended beyond humanity. Martin believed that every animal, no matter how small or unimportant, had intrinsic value since God created it.

One of the most well-known stories about Martin's relationship with animals took place while he was living in a Dominican friary. The friars had long contended with rats and other pests in their kitchen. While most people would have used traps or poison to get rid of the problem, Martin chose a more spiritual approach. He asked the rats to leave in God's name, and they magically did. Martin's influence over animals was not confined to pests; he is reported to have been able to tame and speak with the friary's animals. He was often observed speaking gently to the animals in the garden, and they seemed to respond in kind, as if they were under his care and protection.

This special link he had with animals went beyond mere companionship or utility; it was a profound appreciation of their fundamental worth as part of God's creation. Martin saw them as beings worthy of dignity and respect, rather as inferiors or tools for human advantage. He saw in them the same divine spark that existed in all humans, and his treatment of them reflected his respect for God's creation. Martin's acts demonstrated that compassion is offered to all living species, regardless of their ability to reciprocate.

Martin's concern for animals extended to the plants and earth. He was known to be a nature lover, frequently tending to the friary's gardens with great care and respect. He saw nature not as something to exploit but as a living demonstration of God's goodness and creativity. His love for the natural world was a concrete embodiment of his spirituality, since he believed that God's hand could be seen in nature. He frequently used the beauty and order of creation to draw closer to God, seeing the rhythms of nature as a reflection of the divine harmony that regulated the universe.

Martin's commitment to nature was particularly evident when he observed how the animals in the friary, both wild and domesticated, gathered around him during his prayer times. They seemed to be drawn to the tranquility and holiness of his presence. Martin's relationship with the natural environment reflects the profound sense of unity he had with all creation. He lived with the conviction that every aspect of the world, from the smallest insect to the tallest tree, was part of a magnificent, divine plan reflecting God's love and creativity.

Perhaps one of the most astonishing features of Martin's relationship with creation was his ability to incorporate this passion into his daily existence. He did not divide his spirituality into periods of prayer or religious service; rather, every aspect of his life—whether caring for the ill, performing miracles, or ministering to animals—was an act of devotion. His concern for nature was not distinct from his love for God but rather a natural extension of it. Martin's holistic attitude to life taught people around him that love for God and creation are inextricably linked. Loving and caring for the earth's creatures allowed one to participate in God's creative activity while also becoming closer to the Creator.

In today's society, where the environment and animal welfare are frequently considered secondary concerns, Martin's example serves as a poignant reminder of the value of all life. He demonstrates that love for God entails not only caring for humans but also respecting and nourishing the entire web of life, whether it is the human individual, the animal world, or the natural environment. Martin's life and actions show us that living in harmony with creation means living in harmony with God. He reminds us that everything we encounter, every living creature, is a gift from God and deserves our respect, care, and love.

Saint Martin de Porres left a legacy of tremendous love and kindness that transcended human limits. His concern for animals and the environment demonstrates a spirituality that strives to live in peace with all of creation. His life is a magnificent testament to the fact that God's love has no borders and that all of creation, human and non-human alike, deserves to be treated with decency and respect. Martin's love for all creation encourages us to reevaluate how we interact with the environment around us and to adopt a more sympathetic and reverent attitude toward the natural world.

Through his example, we are called to understand the interconnection of all life and to be stewards of God's creation. Saint Martin of Porres' love for animals and nature reminds us that compassion extends not only to humans but to all of God's creatures. By following in his footsteps, we can become more attuned to the divine presence in our surroundings and act as faithful stewards of the beautiful, interconnected world that God has bestowed on us.

Unity and Harmony in Community

Saint Martin de Porres' life was distinguished not only by his personal acts of compassion and holiness but also by the enormous impact he had on his community, where he bridged the deep barriers of race, class, and status that existed in 16th-century Lima. Martin became a living example of the unity that Christ calls all believers to by demonstrating humility, service, and love. His capacity to promote harmony in the midst of societal divide demonstrates the depth of his holiness and the transformational power of his testimony.

Martin's upbringing, impacted by his mixed racial heritage—his father was a Spanish aristocrat and his mother a liberated Black slave—could have contributed to a sense of alienation. Martin experienced hostility from both the Spanish elite and the lower-class indigenous and African communities in a culture profoundly rooted in racial hierarchies and socioeconomic stratifications. Rather than retreating into animosity or withdrawing from the larger community, Martin turned these problems into chances for grace. He exhibited Christ's teachings by recognizing each person—regardless of color, status, or background—as an equal child of God demanding love and respect.

His life at the Dominican Order's Lima convent exemplified the societal differences of his period. Martin's activities, however, instilled a sense of oneness within the friary community. Despite the discrimination that existed throughout the church and society, Martin's humble service to the friars and the destitute crossed class and racial lines. Martin worked as a servant in the convent, preparing food, cleaning, and performing menial jobs that some may have considered beneath him. However, he never regarded these tasks as humiliating. For Martin, every act of service was an opportunity to serve Christ and his brothers, regardless of their status or color.

Martin used his service to bridge the gap between people. His concern for the poor, sick, and underprivileged, particularly enslaved Africans and indigenous people in Lima, contributed to the dismantling of profoundly entrenched societal divisions. The friars and townspeople saw his modest, self-sacrificing personality and grew to admire him for his spiritual gifts and love, rather than his race or social rank. Martin's humility became his greatest advantage, exemplifying the Christian principle that everyone is equal in God's eyes. He could not have been a more powerful witness to Christ's teachings, which rejected his time's societal hierarchy in favor of reaching out to the most hated and downtrodden sections of society.

Martin's example was not one of passive acceptance; rather, he actively pursued peace and harmony. When conflicts erupted among the friars or in the community, Martin was frequently the mediator. His humble approach to conflict resolution, paired with his ability for healing, aided in the healing of rifts and the establishment of reconciliation. People from all walks of life came to appreciate Martin, not because of his social standing but because of his strong devotion to God's love and the well-being of others. His life became a living example of the value of community, reflecting the body of Christ. Martin did more than just tolerate differences; he celebrated them as part of God's diverse creation and worked to bring people together, even if their backgrounds would have otherwise kept them apart.

His interactions with his fellow friars exemplified this togetherness. While some of the more fortunate members of the community may have regarded Martin as inferior due to his ethnic and class background, Martin's demeanor continuously resisted such biases. He was noted for working ceaselessly alongside the more educated and wealthy friars without seeking attention or superiority. Rather, he served them with a gentle and caring spirit, cultivating an environment that fostered togetherness rather than division. His service was motivated by a love for God and humanity rather than an earthly ambition for power or prestige.

Even his miracles and healings frequently had a barrier-breaking effect. For example, when Martin healed someone of a particular race or class, he did it without regard for distinction. He treated everyone who sought his assistance with similar love and care. He represented universal love and respect, which spoke to the hearts of everyone around him, prompting them to view one another with the same love he had demonstrated.

Martin's outreach to Lima's enslaved African population provided a particularly powerful example of his unifying influence. Martin's compassion for Africans and persons of African heritage distinguished him at a period when they were deemed less than human and frequently treated cruelly. He cared for the sick, helped the impoverished, and, most importantly, treated everyone with dignity and respect. He saw them as equal members of the human family, deserving of the same love that Christ demonstrated to everyone. His acts set a precedent for others to follow, breaking down racial barriers and presenting a vision of true Christian generosity and harmony.

Martin's relationships with the impoverished and oppressed proved that Christian unity is about love, respect, and mutual care, not conformity. His witness challenged the stereotypes of the period and urged the church to welcome all of God's children, regardless of socioeconomic status, race, or origin. The community Martin helped to establish was not flawless or free of human nature's flaws, but his activities directed them toward a more perfect unity in Christ, where all individuals are viewed as equally loved by God.

As we meditate on Saint Martin de Porres' legacy, we are reminded that true unity in the Church and society requires more than surface harmony or the absence of dispute. It necessitates an active commitment to loving and serving all people, regardless of their background or status in life. Martin's example encourages us to break down the boundaries that separate us and seek the common tie we share as God's children. His life demonstrates that the route to unity is through love, humility, and service—values that we are still challenged to embody in our own communities today.

Saint Martin de Porres transcended his time's divisions with his deep compassion and service to all people, leaving a legacy that continues to encourage us to seek harmony with one another, as Christ taught. His life demonstrated that, in the body of Christ, all members—regardless of race, class, or status—are called to live in harmony and as equals in the eyes of God. Martin demonstrated that true Christian unity is established not on outward appearances or societal attitudes but on the love we show one another, regardless of our differences.

Patron to the Poor and Forgotten

Even decades after his death, Saint Martin de Porres' life continues to strike a chord with the most disadvantaged and neglected members of society. Martin's love and compassion, despite being born into a world marked by severe class inequalities and racial discrimination, transcended race, class, and social position barriers. Martin became not just a saint but also a strong symbol of hope and dignity for people who are frequently forgotten by the worldwhen he chose to devote his life to serving the poorest of the poor and the most overlooked sections of society.

In Lima, where he grew up, the impoverished were frequently viewed as invisible, with people in positions of power ignoring their needs. The indigenous population, enslaved Africans, and the lower classes were considered inferior, and the wealthy ignored their plight. Nonetheless, it was these people whom Martin dedicated his life to serving. He became a living example of Christ's admonition to care for "the least of these," and his life was a dramatic testimony to the dignity and worth of every human being, regardless of circumstances.

Martin's connection to the poor and forgotten was more than just a charitable act; it was a deep spiritual vocation. His position as a lay brother in the Dominican Order did not afford him the lofty rank or respect that many religious officials in the church do, but it did allow him to minister directly to individuals in great need. While some may have overlooked the sick and needy, Martin recognized the face of Christ in them. He treated everyone with dignity and compassion, viewing them as treasured children of God. His commitment to caring for Lima's poorest was not confined to those who could repay him in any way but also included those who had nothing to offer in return other than their pain and need.

One of the most noticeable characteristics of Martin's poverty ministry was his ability to tear down societal barriers that kept people apart. He did more than just give the poor food, shelter, and medical care; he made them feel seen, heard, and cherished. In an era when slaves and the impoverished were sometimes overlooked, Martin's simple presence served as a reminder of their importance and dignity. His acts of kindness—feeding the hungry, looking to the sick, and caring for the elderly—were as much about validating the worth of their lives as they were about meeting their physical necessities.

He also aimed to empower the impoverished by giving them opportunities to engage in the community. Martin worked relentlessly to establish relationships, forging links of solidarity and mutual respect that fostered a sense of belonging and affection among Lima's most marginalized citizens. His approach was not one of pity or condescension; rather, it was one of collaboration with the impoverished, respecting their inherent dignity and the possibility of holiness in everyone, regardless of socioeconomic status.

Many of Lima's destitute saw Saint Martin as a beacon of hope. He was a reminder that their lives were important. His commitment to them stood in stark contrast to the wealthy class's apathy. Martin's embodiment of Christ's love and care for the underprivileged highlighted the fact that, in God's eyes, no one is beyond redemption or insignificant. Martin's impact on the poor was not just determined by what he did for them but also by how he made them feel recognized and valued. His ministry went beyond physical treatment, touching the hearts and souls of those who had previously been overlooked.

Martin's compassion and concern for the poor and suffering were most apparent during his healing efforts. His reputation as a healer grew across Lima, particularly among the poor, who were frequently victims of illness, injury, and neglect. Martin's medical care extended beyond the physical realm. He realized that healing entailed not just relieving pain and treating sickness but also providing a deeper level of peace that comforted both the spirit and the body. His ministry provided a haven for those suffering from disease or poverty in a world that frequently appeared unconcerned about their suffering.

Furthermore, Saint Martin's healing ministry put him in direct contact with the most marginalized. Martin, who had a strong sensitivity for human suffering, treated everyone equally, regardless of their social standing. However, he kept special compassion for society's most neglected and hated individuals. African slaves, indigenous people, the ill, and outcasts saw Martin as more than a healer; he was also a friend and advocate. His deep awareness of their pain and capacity to provide genuine care made him a living example of Christ's kindness.

Martin's commitment to the downtrodden went beyond Lima's borders. He became a global patron of the oppressed, underprivileged, and forgotten. His canonization by Pope John XXIII in 1962 was a watershed moment in the church's acceptance of the dignity of all persons, particularly those who had been marginalized or put aside. The church saw Saint Martin as a symbol of the Gospel's preferential option for the poor and the call to help the least of these.

Saint Martin de Porres is now recognized as the patron saint of individuals who are marginalized in society. He is a supporter of racial equality, assisting individuals who face discrimination, prejudice, and injustice. His life and example serve as a poignant reminder that true greatness in God's eyes comes not from status or fortune, but from loving and serving others, particularly those in need. Martin's legacy continues to inspire people of all colors and origins to recognize one another's dignity and work toward creating a world that represents Christ's compassion, mercy, and justice.

For those who feel forgotten or disregarded by society, Saint Martin serves as a strong intercessor and reminder that God sees and loves them. He addresses individuals who may believe they are too impoverished, marginalized, or oppressed to have hope. His life exemplifies the idea that in God's kingdom, everyone has a place, and no one is beyond God's mercy and love.

Saint Martin's compassion for the impoverished, his persistent work to uplift those who had been rejected by society, and his unwavering dedication to seeing Christ in all people make him not only a saint, but also a living beacon of hope for the disadvantaged. His example inspires each of us to consider how we might help people who are often neglected, as well as to acknowledge the power of love to change lives. Saint Martin de Porres' legacy lives on as a reminder that no matter how neglected or disregarded we feel, God sees us, loves us, and calls us to be His instruments of mercy.

A Legacy Carved with Love

Saint Martin de Porres' life exemplifies the transformative power of love—love that looks past the surface, transcends societal divides, and penetrates the hearts of those in need. His legacy continues to inspire Catholics around the world, transcending ages and countries and having a tremendous impact on our understanding of compassion, service, and sanctity. Though he lived in the 16th and early 17th centuries, the light of his unselfish love continues to shine brilliantly today, inspiring all who hear his tale to live more fully in Christ's love.

Martin's legacy is built around his ability to love without bounds. Martin was raised in an environment that continually reminded him of his mixed heritage—African and Spanish descent—and experienced what it was like to be rejected and dismissed by society. However, rather than allowing these events to breed hatred or bitterness, he chose to respond with love. His love was not limited to those who were easy to love; it also included the destitute, the sick, the oppressed, and even those who looked down on him. Through his life, he demonstrated that love had the capacity to break down prejudice, class separation, and racial disparities.

One of the most striking features of Martin's love was its radical inclusion. He wasn't merely concerned with those of his own ethnicity or those who could repay him. He sought out the forgotten and despised, treating them with dignity and kindness. Whether it was the African slaves transported to Lima or the indigenous peoples, Martin reached out to those whom others had rejected. He recognized Christ in them and loved them just as Christ would. His actions were more than just charitable; they were a radical manifestation of the gospel, challenging the status quo and inspiring others to embrace limitless love.

This love was not abstract or theoretical; it was profoundly practical and incarnational. Martin lived a life of service, especially to the impoverished, sick, and forgotten. He used his position in the Dominican Order to help people in need, sacrificing personal goals or desires for rank in favor of serving God via the care of others. Martin's life was a living manifestation of the Gospel message, whether he was tending to the sick, comforting the dying, or caring for the destitute. "Whatever you did for one of the least of these brothers and sisters of mine, you did for me" (Matthew 25:40).

Saint Martin's love was also transforming since it spread throughout all of creation. His loving care for animals, nurturing of nature, and recognition of the interdependence of all of God's creation were defining characteristics of his spiritual identity. He saw the divine in all creatures and treated them with the same regard and care as he did his fellow humans. This holistic perspective of love contributed to his reputation as someone with a kind heart for all living creatures, both human and animal.

Saint Martin of Porres' acts of charity left a legacy that extended well beyond the tangible acts of kindness he performed. His life paved the way for others to follow, one in which love is the driving force behind all actions. Today, Martin is revered as the patron saint of social justice, racial equality, and the oppressed. His legacy continues to inspire Catholics all around the world to advocate for the dignity of all people, regardless of race, origin, or socioeconomic standing. His example encourages believers to live a life that displays Christ's love in every interaction and to recognize God's face in those who are suffering.

Martin's memory resonates especially strongly in neighborhoods plagued by racial injustice and poverty. His canonization in 1962, more than 300 years after his death, was a forceful statement by the Church that all persons, regardless of race or status, are valuable in God's eyes. Saint Martin's life speaks to the current struggles for racial and social justice in the modern world, reminding us that as Christians, we are called to see the dignity of all people, especially those in need. His life remains a beacon of hope for the oppressed, a model for those seeking to make a difference in the world through love, and a compelling reminder that the work of justice is inextricably linked to the call to love.

Martin's impact extends beyond those suffering from poverty and injustice to the lives of regular Catholics. His tale is about devotion to prayer, service, and the gospel. His profound prayer life, unshakeable faith in God's providence, and modest service continue to inspire Catholics all around the world. Martin's life is a source of hope for individuals who are struggling with personal problems, illness, or societal constraints, demonstrating that holiness can be discovered in the most humble circumstances and that a life of love and service is always possible, regardless of one's social status.

Martin's impact is also found in the Dominican Order, where he was a devoted member. His example of humility, generosity, and devotion has continued to influence the Order's identity, urging both Dominican friars and laypeople to follow in his footsteps of selfless service and deep prayer. In many respects, Martin represents the Dominican charism of preaching through action, demonstrating that the gospel must be lived out in acts of kindness and compassion as much as through words.

Saint Martin de Porres is also a saint of persons seeking spiritual as well as physical recovery. His capacity to perform miraculous healings was more than just a manifestation of his heavenly connection; it also represented the healing power of love and kindness. Just as Martin cared for the sick and the underprivileged, his life serves as a reminder that our love has the capacity to heal the world's wounds. Every act of compassion, every moment of charity, allows us to bring Christ's healing touch to those who are suffering.

Ultimately, Saint Martin de Porres left a legacy of love in action. His example invites us to embody Christ's love in our own lives, to reach out to those in need, and to create a world in which everyone is respected and cared for. Martin's modest yet powerful acts of love have left a legacy that continues to inspire millions around the world, reminding us of the power of love to change lives and impact the world.

In a society currently plagued by conflict, bigotry, and inequity, Saint Martin de Porres' life stands as a remarkable testament to the transformational power of God's love. His legacy serves as a reminder that true greatness in the eyes of God is found in modest service to others, particularly those in most need. His life demonstrates that love is more than a sentiment; it is an activity, a way of life, capable of changing the world one act of mercy at a time. His example invites us to travel the road of love, to serve others as Christ did, and to create a world that represents God's compassion, justice, and mercy.

CANONIZATION AND THE MODERN DEVOTION TO ST. MARTIN

The Journey to Sainthood

Saint Martin de Porres' route to canonization was long, marked by years of prayer, devotion, and miracles that validated his life's holiness. His canonization not only recognized a life well lived, but also confirmed his great impact on the Church, his community, and the globe. Martin lived a life of humility, love, and service, and it took many centuries for the Church to officially recognize him as a saint—a process that demonstrates the enduring power of his example.

Martin de Porres passed away on November 3, 1639, following years of dedicated service to the sick, destitute, and oppressed in Lima, Peru. Although he was well acknowledged for his holiness during his lifetime, the Catholic Church did not begin the formal process of canonization until centuries after his death. This delay was not uncommon, as many saints' causes take time to develop. Martin envisioned a gradual acceptance of his holiness, culminating in his beatification and canonization in the twentieth century.

Martin was beatified, which was the first step toward canonization. The Catholic Church officially began the process of beatification for Martin in 1837. Beatification is a phase in the canonization process that acknowledges a person's entry into heaven and ability to intercede for others on earth. It is a significant step toward full sainthood because it recognizes that the individual is "blessed" and has lived a life of heroic virtue. The process of beatification frequently include gathering testimony about the person's life and miracles, researching their virtues, and validating any accounts of intercessory miracles after death.

The Vatican thoroughly researched Martin's life and heard countless accounts from individuals who knew him and others who had been affected by his miracles. His life of service to the impoverished, amazing healings, and miracles ascribed to his intercession were instrumental in furthering his cause. Martin's humility, devotion to prayer, and unmatched care for the sick and impoverished were carefully chronicled, and witness testimonials of his holiness added to the evidence.

After the examination was concluded and Martin was proclaimed "venerable" in 1837, the next step was beatification. This happened on May 9, 1837, when Pope Gregory XVI officially beatified Martin de Porres. This was a historic occasion, since the Church recognized Martin as a model of holiness. His beatification was warmly hailed, particularly in Latin America and among the Dominicans, who benefited enormously from his example of humility and service.

Martin had been recognized as "blessed," but the final step toward canonization remained. Canonization is the final recognition that a person is actually in heaven and deserves universal reverence by the faithful. This step needs the verification of at least two miracles attributed to the candidate's intercession after beatification. The Church carefully reviewed the miracles that contributed to Martin's canonization, and their acceptance was critical in completing his route to sainthood.

One of the most remarkable miracles ascribed to Saint Martin occurred in 1950, when a small kid suffering from a life-threatening disease was said to have been healed via Martin's prayer. Medical authorities confirmed this healing, which was one of the miracles that helped advance Martin's cause. His canonization process accelerated following this miracle, ending in his final recognition.

On May 6, 1962, Pope John XXIII declared Martin de Porres a saint of the Church. The canonization was crucial not only for Peru and the Dominican Order, but for the entire Catholic Church. It was the time when Martin's example of humility, service, and love was recognized as a model for all Christians. His canonization was hailed by the impoverished, the sick, and everyone who had been touched by his kindness over the ages.

The canonization of Saint Martin de Porres recognized his life's everlasting relevance and strong relationship to God. It was an admission that his style of life—characterized by compassion, humility, and concern for the marginalized—was a model of Christian holiness. His life was characterized by humble, loving service to people in need rather than grandeur or worldly achievement. The Church regarded this life as worthy of emulation by all of its members.

Martin de Porres' canonization was a victory not only for the saint, but also for the underprivileged populations he had diligently served. His canonization sent a striking message: sainthood is not reserved for the powerful or those of high social rank, but rather for people who live out the Gospel with humility, compassion, and a genuine love for God and others. Martin's life reminds us that everyone, regardless of social level, has the capacity to become a saint if they live with love and dedication to God.

Today, Saint Martin de Porres represents a beacon of hope for all people, particularly those who experience injustice or discrimination. His canonization reaffirmed the Church's commitment to upholding the dignity of all people, regardless of race, class, or background. Martin's sainthood also reflected the Church's expanding emphasis on social justice and caring for the poor and oppressed. His canonization occurred during a period of significant social change, particularly in the 1960s, and his legacy continues to inspire movements for racial and social justice around the world.

In conclusion, Saint Martin de Porres' route to sainthood was long, but it was well worth the wait. His example of service, humility, and love for the marginalized speaks volumes to the Church today. His canonization in 1962 marked the end of a process that acknowledged his remarkable sanctity, deep love for God and humanity, and long-lasting influence on the Church and the world. His example reminds us that sainthood is about living a life of love and service, not prestige or acclaim, and that true holiness can be discovered in simple, humble actions of caring for others. The canonization of Saint Martin de Porres continues to inspire future generations of Catholics to follow in his footsteps of mercy and compassion, leaving an eternal legacy of love for the world.

Celebrating the Feast Day of St. Martin

The Feast Day of St. Martin de Porres, celebrated on November 3rd each year, is a joyful occasion for Catholics around the world, particularly in Latin America, where his life and legacy resonate deeply. His feast day serves not only as a remembrance of his holiness but also as an opportunity to reflect on the virtues he embodied—humility, charity, and a deep love for the poor and marginalized. It is a day to celebrate his life of service and spread his compassionate example via prayers, processions, and charity gestures.

Throughout the world, the Feast of St. Martin has evolved into a celebration of both faith and community. The day begins with somber Masses and ends with celebrations that highlight Martin's strong commitment to the poor, love for all creation, and long-lasting impact on the lives of the faithful. These commemorations are not just actions of reverence, but also of solidarity, drawing attention to the continuous work of compassion and mercy that Martin advocated throughout his life.

St. Martin's feast day is particularly important in Peru, where he spent much of his life. Lima, where he performed his humble ministry, becomes a focal place for public shows of devotion. People congregate in the Plaza de Armas, the city's largest square, where the Convento de Santo Domingo, a Dominican Order church, stands as a reminder of his legacy. The church frequently holds special liturgies, processions, and meetings to commemorate the life of St. Martin, with the faithful praying for the saint's continuous intercession.

During these festivities, many participants emphasize Martin's ongoing significance to the struggles of the oppressed. The impoverished and sick, who were always at the center of Martin's ministry, are especially honored on this day. Some churches provide food, clothing, or medical supplies to the most poor, mirroring Martin's charity efforts throughout his life. This practice reflects Martin's Dominican beliefs of serving the poor, the sick, and those in need of mercy. Through these gestures of kindness, the faithful not only memorialize Martin's memory, but also renew their commitment to helping the needy.

The devotion to St. Martin de Porres is also characterized by the sharing of legends about his miracles and the ongoing impact of his intercession. These stories are shared in churches, homes, and even on social media platforms, as individuals from all over the world recount how Martin's intercession has brought them healing, peace, and hope. The recounting of these miraculous events allows the faithful to connect intimately with the saint, feeling a sense of closeness and intimacy with a figure who walked the earth with tremendous humility and love.

In nations such as the United States, where devotion to St. Martin has expanded in recent decades, the feast day has served as an opportunity to bring disparate groups together. Many African American Catholics, in particular, have a unique devotion to St. Martin, viewing him as a saint who fought bigotry and racial discrimination, just as they confront comparable challenges in their own lives. St. Martin's Day is celebrated culturally in places such as New York, Chicago, and Los Angeles, with musical performances, processions, and fellowship events that bring people from all ethnicities and races together in a shared expression of religion.

The Feast of St. Martin is celebrated with reverence and delight in Dominican communities all throughout the world, particularly in the United States. These communities celebrate special Masses in honor of their brother, who, despite humble origins, became an exemplar of Dominican spirituality and a model for the Order's mission of preaching and aiding the poor. Hymns are sung at Masses, thanksgiving prayers are offered, and the Dominican rosary is recited in honor of the saint.

The emphasis on St. Martin's love of animals is one of the feast day celebrations' distinguishing features. Martin, known for caring for God's creation, is frequently represented surrounded by animals such as cats, dogs, and even birds. to his feast day, it is not uncommon to bestow blessings to animals in churches or households, emphasizing Martin's strong connection to nature. Many Catholic communities have "Blessing of the Animals" services on or around November 3rd, a custom that celebrates his compassion for animals and his belief that all creation is deserving of care and respect.

In the Philippines, another country where devotion to St. Martin is spreading, parishes dedicated to his memory frequently stage colorful processions. These processions often include images and statues of St. Martin that are carried through the streets while the devout sing hymns and pray. The celebrations are joyful and reverent, emphasizing Martin's deep relationship to the Divine and his persistent service to the impoverished and suffering.

In many regions, particularly in Central and South America, feast days are used to showcase the region's cultural richness. The different St. Martin's Day festivals frequently incorporate traditional dances, music, and food, reflecting the rich cultural legacy of the communities that commemorate him. These cultural events provide an opportunity to emphasize how the Catholic faith is connected with local customs and values in each region.

While the Feast of St. Martin de Porres is a season of joy and celebration, it also provides an opportunity for reflection. In many parishes, the day is celebrated as a chance to renew one's commitment to living a life of service to others, as Martin did. The faithful are urged to reflect on their own lives and consider how they can more thoroughly embody Martin's virtues of charity, humility, and compassion. As students join in Masses, processions, and charitable deeds, they are reminded that the genuine celebration of St. Martin's life lies not in spectacular gestures, but in little acts of love and service that emulate Christ.

The Feast of St. Martin de Porres is celebrated around the world as a day of joy, unity, and profound spiritual connection. It is a day to honor a saint who conquered adversity and prejudice, and whose life exemplified the power of love, humility, and service. As the faithful gather to commemorate his life and miracles, they are reminded that the route to holiness lies in the ordinary, everyday acts of caring for others and serving the marginalized—as St. Martin did throughout his life. Through these commemorations, his legacy lives on, motivating everyone who wish to follow in his footsteps and pursue lives of compassionate service to the world.

Miracles of St. Martin Today

St. Martin de Porres, who dedicated his life to helping the poor, sick, and disenfranchised, not only left a legacy of compassion and service, but he continues to inspire and work marvels even after his death. His canonization as a saint in 1962 recognized his holiness during his lifetime, but since then, other reports of miraculous healings and divine interventions ascribed to his intercession have emerged. These modern-day miracles demonstrate the ongoing power of his prayers and his close relationship to the Heavenly Father.

One of the most striking elements of the miracles credited to St. Martin's intercession is the constancy with which they occur. These wonders, like his life, tend to revolve around themes of healing, alleviation from pain, and the empowerment of those in desperate need. Stories of miraculous recoveries from illness, financial provisions during difficult times, and even unexplained protections from harm continue to circulate among the faithful, cementing St. Martin's reputation as a saint who walks among his people, offering hope and interceding on their behalf.

1. **Miracle Healings**

Perhaps the most common miracle credited to St. Martin's intercession is the curing of physical illnesses. People continue to turn to him in hospitals, homes, and towns where his devotion is strong. Accounts of people recovering unexpectedly from chronic or life-threatening illnesses are prevalent. One of the most well-known cases involves a woman from Lima, Peru, who was diagnosed with terminal cancer. After praying to St. Martin for intercession, she reported that her doctors had found no trace of the sickness, contrary to their prior prediction. This amazing recovery, which has been shared by many in the community, continues to inspire the faithful to turn to St. Martin in times of need.

In various regions of the world, people who are suffering from mental and emotional distress report receiving miraculous alleviation after invoking the saint's name. One particularly moving tale comes from a family in the United States who had been dealing with a loved one's serious depression. Despite months of therapy and medicine, the family's prayers to St. Martin for peace were answered when the individual demonstrated a dramatic and sustained recovery in both emotional and psychological health. Such narratives are interpreted as evidence of St. Martin's tremendous compassion for those who suffer, mirroring his own life spent ministering to the suffering and downtrodden.

Protection and Provision

Another theme that has evolved in contemporary miracle accounts is that of heavenly protection and provision, particularly in times of extreme need. People recount strange occurrences of safety following accidents or near-disasters after calling on St. Martin for help. In one particularly dramatic case, a man was involved in an automobile accident on a rainy night. Despite the severity of the disaster, he escaped unhurt, subsequently crediting his miraculous survival to St. Martin's protection. In gratitude, he shared his experience with his local parish, where many others have since given similar accounts of being spared harm after praying to St. Martin.

Equally compelling are claims of money miracles linked to the saint. Individuals who have experienced severe poverty or financial despair recall instances in which, after invoking St. Martin's name, they got unexpected financial assistance or resources. One woman described how, after losing her job and struggling to pay for her family, she prayed to St. Martin for help.

The following day, she got an anonymous donation that paid her bills for the month. While the circumstances of the donation are unknown, she believes it was a direct response to her prayer and a symbol of St. Martin's continuous concern for the needs of the faithful.

Bring People Together

The miracles credited to St. Martin today might be spiritual as well as physical or material in nature. Many people have reported feeling peaceful and reconciled in their relationships after asking St. Martin's intercession. His life was dedicated to breaking barriers, whether racial, social, or economic, and many modern-day miracles reflect his continued efforts to bring people together who had previously been estranged. A married couple, for example, revealed how their relationship had deteriorated owing to years of miscommunication and animosity. When they began praying to St. Martin for healing in their relationship, they observed an immediate shift in their attitudes toward one another, with renewed compassion and understanding entering their hearts. These emotional healings, while less evident, are powerfully felt, leading many people to consider St. Martin as a healer of both bodies and hearts.

A Global Legacy.

St. Martin's miracles continue to be reported over the world, and his reputation as a strong intercessor for the poor, sick, and downtrodden remains unshaken. Whether in the bustling capitals of Latin America, the peaceful rural parts of North America, or in towns all over Europe, the faithful continue to turn to St. Martin in times of need. Modern miracles have also increased interest in his life and legacy, often resulting in new devotions and prayers to the saint in areas where his name was previously unknown.

For example, in some African communities, St. Martin has come to represent optimism in the midst of poverty and hardship. Devotees recount miracles of provision, healing, and release from life-threatening situations, attributing these events to the saint's strong intervention. Stories of miraculous protection during times of civil turmoil or famine have bolstered his reputation as a champion of the oppressed. In such regions, the Feast of St. Martin is observed with zeal, not only as a religious observance but also as a moment to remember his constant concern for the suffering and his ongoing miracles in the world today.

St. Martin de Porres, the modest Dominican brother who lived among the poor and ministered with a loving heart, is still working in the lives of many people via the numerous miracles credited to his intercession. His legacy consists not just of piety and good works but also of actual acts of divine love that spread over generations. For those who see his miracles, whether via miraculous healings, unexpected provisions, or supernatural protection, St. Martin continues to be a living witness to God's love and mercy in the world.

Through these modern miracles, St. Martin de Porres shows the faithful that holiness is not limited to the past but rather thrives in the lives of those who call on him with trust. His life of service and love continues to be a light of hope, reminding us all that God's kindness knows no bounds—not even time or place.

A Model of Faith for Our Time

St. Martin de Porres, the humble and compassionate Dominican brother, remains a shining example of faith for Catholics and people from all walks of life today. His life, founded on love for God and service to others, teaches profound teachings that transcend time and place. In a society that is frequently fragmented, divided, and plagued with suffering, St. Martin's example of unity, compassion, and selfless commitment to the downtrodden speaks directly to the needs of today's followers. His life serves as a reminder that true holiness is found not in rank or fortune but in quiet service to others and humility, which recognizes God as the source of all good.

1. **Accepting the Call to Serve.**

In an age when many people are burdened by the pressures of career, societal expectations, and personal ambition, St. Martin's life teaches us that greatness is found in humble service, not in recognition or power. Martin's life indicates that true discipleship transcends human barriers of race, class, and rank. Born from an impoverished, mixed-race household, Martin has personally seen the discrimination and struggle that many people confront today. Despite these hurdles, he never let them prevent him from fulfilling his calling to serve people with compassion.

Today, as the world grapples with issues of poverty, racism, and injustice, St. Martin's example provides a blueprint for how we might all contribute to a more equitable and compassionate society. His dedication to serving the ill, the impoverished, and the disadvantaged teaches us that each human life is infinitely valuable in God's eyes. Whether we are helping the homeless in our towns, working with the sick in hospitals, or assisting marginalized populations, Martin's life encourages us to open our hearts to those in need, seeing Christ in everyone of them and responding with love and action.

The Value of Compassion and Forgiveness

St. Martin's example of unconditional love and forgiveness challenges the skepticism and division that so often exist in our world today. His unwavering compassion for others, even those who treated him with contempt, demonstrates the power of mercy. In an era when social media and public conversation frequently promote division and enmity, St. Martin's life challenges us to see past our differences and choose forgiveness and understanding over wrath and retribution.

His forgiveness extended to people who discriminated against him because of his mixed ethnicity and low socioeconomic level. He experienced prejudice and marginalization from society, yet he refused to become bitter. Instead, he prayed for those who insulted or mistreated him, forgiving them with the same kindness he showed to the sick and the impoverished. In our own lives, we are frequently faced with the choice between forgiveness and resentment. St. Martin's example encourages us to choose mercy, as Christ did, and to forgive those who have harmed us—not because they deserve it, but because we are all God's children, called to love one another as He loves us.

Holiness in Everyday Life.

In a world that frequently rewards great accomplishments and obvious success, St. Martin's life tells us that holiness can be found in regular moments of life. He didn't live a lavish lifestyle. In truth, he often worked in the background, supporting others without seeking praise. His healing hands, compassion for animals, and devotion to prayer were all gestures of kindness performed discreetly and without fanfare. He worked as a barber and lived among the poor, carrying out his daily responsibilities with humility and care, all while leading a life of intense spiritual commitment.

This message is especially vital in our current society, where the chase of success, fortune, and fame frequently trumps the fundamental command to live authentically and serve others. In our hectic lives, it's easy to forget the importance of regular duties. However, St. Martin's life reminds us to seek holiness in whatever we do, no matter how small or trivial it may appear. Whether we are working in our workplaces, caring for children at home, or supporting a neighbor in need, every act can be used to serve God and others. With love and devotion, the ordinary can become remarkable.

The Need for Unity in a Divided World.

Saint Martin's life exemplifies the profound need for unity in a divided world. Political polarization, racial conflicts, and socioeconomic inequalities have created a climate in which it might be difficult to overcome social barriers. However, St. Martin's life demonstrates the possibility of unity within variety. He was a man who, through his devotion and humility, drew people together from all races, social classes, and economic backgrounds. He lived a life that demonstrated how loving and serving others, regardless of background, may foster a link of unity based on faith and love.

St. Martin's ability to overcome racial biases of his period poses a challenge to modern civilization. His actions, not his words, prompted change. He welcomed people from different backgrounds, bringing them together through acts of love and compassion. His example encourages us to evaluate our own prejudices and biases and take active actions to promote unity in our homes, churches, and communities. We, too, are asked to break down the barriers that separate us and work toward reconciliation, as St. Martin did in his day.

A Saint of the Marginalized and Poor

As we face tremendous difficulties in poverty, injustice, and inequality, St. Martin de Porres remains a potent patron of the marginalized. His profound empathy for the impoverished and sick reflects his belief that God's heart beats for those on the edges. His life encourages us to go outside our comfort zones and engage with those who are sometimes overlooked by society. As St. Martin's life demonstrates, the obligation to serve the poor is more than just a duty; it is also a route to holiness.

St. Martin's commitment to the impoverished serves as a reminder that Christ's call to care for "the least of these" remains eternal. In a world that frequently idolizes riches, power, and reputation, St. Martin's life is a sharp contrast. He demonstrated that true greatness is found not in gaining wealth or position but in caring for those who have none. His example encourages us to consider how we can more thoroughly accept the Gospel invitation to assist the impoverished and oppressed in our own communities, knowing that by doing so, we are serving Christ himself.

A Call to Action.

St. Martin de Porres is an enduring example of what it means to live a life of faith, love, and service. His life teaches us that holiness is not limited to the remarkable but may be found in the most ordinary acts of compassion and caring. In a world that frequently feels alienated, divided, and overwhelmed by suffering, St. Martin's example encourages us to reconnect to the essence of the gospel: to love God with all our hearts and to love our neighbors, particularly those in need, as ourselves.

As we face contemporary concerns such as racial justice, poverty, illness, and societal division, St. Martin's life continues to speak to us. He invites us to embody an active, caring, and transformative faith rather than a passive or theoretical one. He reminds us that by serving others, we encounter Christ and experience the true joy of living our faith. May his example of humility, compassion, and commitment inspire us to carry out our call to love and serve in the world today.

Printed in Great Britain
by Amazon